A Mother's Love

TO MOM

Thanks for listening
Thanks for caring
Thanks for always helping
    in times of need
Thanks for sharing
Thanks Mom,
    for always being there

—Miles M. Hutchinson

Other books by

Blue Mountain Press INC.

Come Into the Mountains, Dear Friend
by Susan Polis Schutz
I Want to Laugh, I Want to Cry
by Susan Polis Schutz
Peace Flows from the Sky
by Susan Polis Schutz
Someone Else to Love
by Susan Polis Schutz
I'm Not That Kind of Girl
by Susan Polis Schutz
Yours If You Ask
by Susan Polis Schutz
Love, Live and Share
by Susan Polis Schutz
The Best Is Yet to Be
Step to the Music You Hear, Vol. I
The Language of Friendship
The Language of Love
The Language of Happiness
The Desiderata of Happiness
by Max Ehrmann
I Care About Your Happiness
by Kahlil Gibran/Mary Haskell
I Wish You Good Spaces
Gordon Lightfoot
We Are All Children Searching for Love
by Leonard Nimoy
Come Be with Me
by Leonard Nimoy
Catch Me with Your Smile
by Peter McWilliams
Creeds to Love and Live By
On the Wings of Friendship
Think of Me Kindly
by Ludwig van Beethoven
You've Got a Friend
Carole King
With You There and Me Here
I Want You to Be Happy
by Hoyt Axton
The Dawn of Friendship
Once Only
by jonivan
Expressing Our Love
Just the Way I Am
Dolly Parton
You and Me Against the World
Paul Williams
What the World Needs Now Is Love
Hal David/Burt Bacharach
Words of Wisdom, Words of Praise
Reach Out for Your Dreams
gentle freedom, gentle courage
diane westlake
A Friend Forever

A Mother's Love

a collection of poems

edited by
Susan Polis Schutz

Blue Mountain Press ™

Boulder, Colorado

Library of Congress Number: 80-67488
ISBN: 0-88396-122-9

Manufactured in the United States of America
First Printing: October, 1980

Thanks to the Blue Mountain Arts creative staff, with special thanks to Douglas Pagels and Faith Hamilton.

ACKNOWLEDGMENTS are on page 64

Blue Mountain Press INC.

P.O. Box 4549, Boulder, Colorado 80306

CONTENTS

A Mother's Love

A special kind of love
that's always there when you need it
to comfort and inspire,
yet lets you go your own path.
A sharing heart
filled with patience and forgiveness,
that takes your side
even when wrong.
Nothing can take its place.

—Debra Colin-Cooke

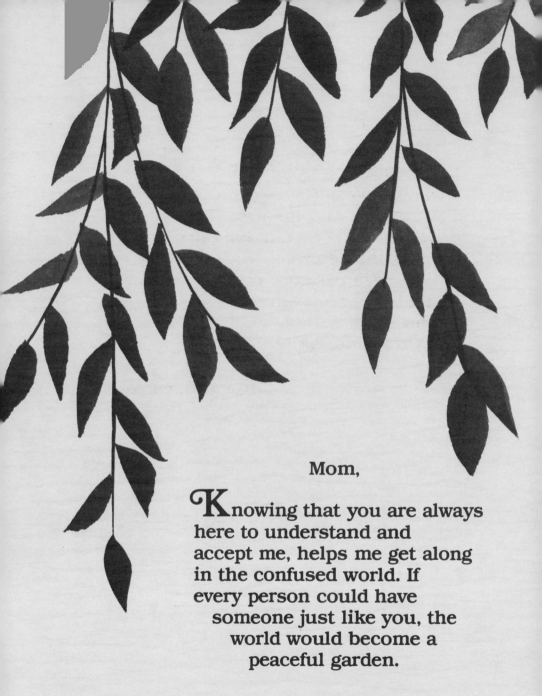

Mom,

Knowing that you are always
here to understand and
accept me, helps me get along
in the confused world. If
every person could have
someone just like you, the
world would become a
peaceful garden.

—Susan Polis Schutz

Every thing in nature bespeaks the mother. The sun is the mother of the earth and gives it its nourishment of heat; it never leaves the universe at night until it has put the earth to sleep to the song of the sea and the hymn of the birds and brooks. And this earth is the mother of trees and flowers. It produces them, nurses them, and weans them. The trees and flowers become kind mothers of their great fruits and seeds. And the mother, the prototype of all existence, is the eternal spirit, full of beauty and love.

—Kahlil Gibran

Throughout our lives
as we count our successes
and pat ourselves on the back,
how seldom do we remember
who it was that began it all.
I was very fortunate
in God's decision
that I be given to the woman
I now know as my mother,
for it was she who showed me
how to care, how to love,
how to feel, and how to be free.

—James Bruce Joseph Sievers

Mother

My love for you
is deep and unalterable.
In me, the memory
of your goodness and devotion
will never fade.
I should like to find words
to prove to you
how much I love you,
how my heart is filled
to overflowing with reverence
and gratitude
to you.

—Franz Liszt

Thank You, Mom

Gratitude is the hardest
of all emotions to express.
There is no word capable of
conveying all that one feels.
Until we reach a world
where thoughts can be adequately
expressed in words,
"thank you" will have to do.

—A. P. Gouthey

You have always been there
when I needed you.
Even though we don't always agree
with each other,
our love has always prevailed.
You have taught me kindness
and understanding—
you have given me the ability
to find love in the world.

—Andrew Harding Allen

$\mathcal{A}$ mother represents all the patience and forgiveness that are needed for support throughout one's life.

—Debra Colin-Cooke

Dear Mother,
You will never know
how much I love you . . .
God bless you and keep you,
and my love to you
every minute and always.

—Richard Davis

$\mathcal{F}$orever is the love
that is filled with understanding
Forever is the love
that is true and undemanding
Forever is the love
that can stand the test of time.
Forever I am yours . . .

—Dolly Parton

$\mathcal{I}$ have never met anybody in my life, I think, who loved his mother as much as I love you. I don't believe there ever was anybody who did, quite so much, and quite in so many wonderful ways.

—Edna St. Vincent Millay

To Mother

Whenever you are
happy, I am happy, too
because you
are an important part of me
and my life is
intermingled with your
life.
I love you.

—Susan Polis Schutz

All that I am
or hope to be
I owe to my mother.

—Abraham Lincoln

My dear mother . . .
if you are happy,
I have everything
I can wish for.

—Thomas Moore

The best and most beautiful
things in the world
cannot be seen
or even touched.
They must be felt
with the heart.

—Helen Keller

A Mother's Heart

$\mathcal{A}$ mother's heart
holds the fondest memories,
the noblest dreams
for her child.
I am grateful when
I think
of your loving heart,
Mother.
Thanks for letting go
yet clasping me always
to your loving heart.

—Jean Therese Lynch

To Mother

Our HOME is the place where I
first learned to love and where I
first learned to share.

Our HOME is the place where there is a
person who always cares.

Even if I am far away, the memory of
our HOME remains close in my heart.

—Andrew Harding Allen

$\mathcal{M}$any make the household
but only one the home.

—James Russell Lowell

Thinking of home
Thinking of the past
Thinking of tomorrow
Brings me closer to you
You are a special person
who brings lasting joy
into my life

—Louise Bradford Lowell

God could not
be everywhere,
so he created
mothers.

—Jewish proverb

Never, dear Mother
shall I be able to
thank you enough
for helping me
to so much happiness.

—Francis Joseph I

Mothers are the daughters
of yesterday,
the grandmothers of tomorrow
and the hope of today.

Mothers are the closest to God
one can feel while passing through
this world's great story.

—Edith Schaffer Lederberg

$\mathcal{M}$any joys
have touched me through my mother . . .
I've been going through old photographs,
   and pictures I drew in 1st grade,
      my first baby teeth,
         a lock of hair . . .
all the tender, special memories
my Mother saved,
and I smile
and feel warm inside.

Now I'm collecting the treasures
   of my own children . . .
I pray some day they will sort through these,
   and remember . . .
      and smile . . .
         and feel warm inside.

—Sue Mitchell

For Mother

When someone cares
it is easier to speak
it is easier to listen
it is easier to play
it is easier to work

When someone cares
it is easier to laugh

—Susan Polis Schutz

When I think of your loving face,
and of how pleasant it is
to live with you,
of your deep serenity,
your charming tranquility,
I know very well that
I shall never love anyone
as much as you.

—Gustave Flaubert

I search among the plain
   and lovely words
To find what the one word
   "Mother" means . . .

"Mother"—a word that holds
   the tender spell
Of all the dear essential
   things of earth;
A home, clean sunlit rooms,
   and the good smell
Of bread; a table spread;
   a glowing hearth.
And love beyond
   the dream of anyone . . .
I search for words for her . . .
   and there are none.

—Grace Noll Crowell

Mothers

God made mothers more special than anyone else. He made them the bearers of life and in so doing, knew they had to be more exceptional than the rest of us. He made them the cornerstone of the home, the foundation of the family, the backbone of society, the ideal of all that is best with the human race. They are the guardians of decency, the preservers of peace, the upholders of truth, the protectors of morality, the symbol of virtue, an inspiration to all that is noble and good in life, and love knows no greater representative than that of a mother's love. Upon our earth, no title is more revered and no sound more beautiful or sweeter heard than the tender loving word—mother.

—Daniel Haughian

Mother is the name
for God
in the lips and hearts
of little children.

—William Makepeace Thackeray

What a wonderful thing
  is a mother!
Other folks can love you,
  but only your mother understands;
She works for you—
  looks after you—
Loves you, forgives you . . .

—Baroness von Hutton

She is just an extraordinary
mother and a gentle person.
I depended on her for everything . . .
I watched her become
a strong person,
and that had an enormous
influence on me.

—Rosalynn Carter

$\mathbf{I}$t seems God moves about her
more freely than he does most people,
and that the soul of Mother
is in some way so familiar
with His presence that
she doesn't think to title
their relationship.

—Joan Baez

Mom

The hardest job has gone to you
To you who means the most to me
You've always been there
   to pick me up
   and guide me
There to scream and yell
   or to sit and listen
You've shared my happiness
   my love
   my sickness
   and health

You've felt pride
   and disappointment

Most of all,
   you've loved me
   and always will

—Donna Elker

Time cannot change . . .
　　a warm sunrise in the
　　　　morning
　　children playing in the fields
　　a sea gull soaring in the sky
　　the honest curiosity of a child
Time cannot change
　　the kindness and
　　　　understanding of
　　a Mother's love

—Joel Winsome Williams

The more I experience life
the more I realize
That a mother as great as you
is really very rare.

—Andrew Harding Allen

If she hadn't been there to
support and encourage me, I
might not have grown up to
be the confident person I am.

—Marlo Thomas

A Mother's Love . . .

Love that is always there
        when you need it
Love that knows all
        your needs
Love that comforts when
        you feel sad
Love that is generous
        and patient
Love that is more understanding
        with every passing year

—Virginia Leigh Robbins

I must tell you how much
I love you; that with each day
I learn to extol your love
and your worth more—
and that when I look back
over my life, I can find nothing
in your treatment of me
that I would alter.

I believe, most beloved mother,
that the improvement of the world
can only arise when mothers
like you are increased
thousands of times
and have more children.

—Louis D. Brandeis

A special thought
for you, Mom

We all need
a person to understand
Someone to share our
thoughts with
and always be around
in time of need
We all need
a person like you

—Louise Bradford Lowell

I hope, my own dear mother,
that you are as well
and happy at home
as my heart wishes you to be.

—Thomas Moore

I keep thinking
about you
every few minutes
all day.

—Walt Whitman

My dear Mother, the growth
of a lifetime is not cut down by
absence . . . let me tell you as
earnestly and gladly as I can,
that I never loved you so
devotedly as I do this
moment. That every day on
which I have delayed to write,
you have been before
my eyes . . .

That in my happiest hours,
my happiness has been
incomplete without you.

—Edmund Clarence Stedman

Of your love I am always so sure
that it needed no such kind words
as you write to assure me
of my precious possession of it.
But it is good to feel it come
so near me.

—Lincoln Steffens

Mother

She showed me how to love
  when I thought I knew how
She was there to kiss away
  the tears when I was hurt
She was there to let me try my wings
  and help the hurt go away
  when things didn't go the way
  I had planned
She was there with her love
  to make me feel special
She was there with
  her knowledge and wisdom
  when I faced a new experience
I pray that when I am lucky enough
  to become a mother, I will be
  as kind and as loving as mine

—Donna Wayland

To Mom

What greater thing is there
for two human souls
than to feel that they are
joined for life—
to strengthen each other
in all labor,
to rest on each other
in all sorrow,
to minister to each other
in all pain,
and to be with each other
in silent unspeakable memories . . .

—George Eliot

Thinking of you,
Mother

The happiness that families share
is the greatest joy in the world.
The knowledge that there is always someone
who cares is a treasure nothing can match.
The love of a family
makes life beautiful.

—Andrew Harding Allen

Mother darling,

It is wonderful to meet
and talk over everything
and share and laugh
and understand each other's situations
as no one else can.

—Anne Morrow Lindbergh

Dear Mother

You know that nothing
can ever change
what we have always been
and always will be
to each other.

—Franklin Delano Roosevelt

total filling and flooding
of body and heart
in the silence of the mother's embrace
transcending all other forms of feeling
touching the higher realms
of comfort . . . safety . . . surrender
floating gently in the ethers
of the universal womb
simple and complete knowing
you have been brought to . . .
and . . . now . . . are held closely within
the soft and constant bosom
of mother love

—diane westlake

For all you have done
  for the gifts you have given
For the love you have shown
  in the life we are living

I thank you
with the whole of my heart.

—Andrew Tawney

To my Mother:
My help and my inspiration,
the one who has had
faith in me always
and who has stood by me
in brightest day and darkest night.
To my only sweetheart,
my Mother.

—Octavus Roy Cohen

My sentiments remain the
same . . . the feeling of thanks
for that grand love of yours
towards your child, which you
displayed so warmly and so
tenderly.

—Richard Wagner

My ever-loved Mother,
I salute you with my affection
once more, and thank you
for bringing me into this world,
and for all your unwearied
care over me there.
May God reward you for it—
as assuredly He will
and does.

—Thomas Carlyle

Since I have a mother
whose many interests
keep her excited and occupied

Since I have a mother
who interacts with so many people
that she has a real feeling for
the world

Since I have a mother
who always is strong
through any period of suffering

Since I have a mother
who is a complete person
I always have a model
to look up to
and that makes it easier
for me to develop into
an independent person
Thanks, Mom

—Susan Polis Schutz

ACKNOWLEDGMENTS

We gratefully acknowledge the permission granted by the following authors, publishers and authors' representatives to reprint poems and excerpts from their publications.

Harcourt Brace Jovanovich, Inc. for "Mother darling," by Anne Morrow Lindbergh. From the book THE FLOWER AND THE NETTLE. Copyright © 1976 by Anne Morrow Lindbergh. All rights reserved. Reprinted by permission.

Donna Wayland for "Mother." Copyright © Donna Wayland, 1978. All rights reserved. Reprinted by permission.

The Viking Press, Inc. for "I must tell you how much," by Louis D. Brandeis. From the book BRANDEIS: A FREE MAN'S LIFE, by Alpheus Thomas Mason. Copyright © 1946 by Alpheus Thomas Mason; reprinted by permission of the publisher, The Viking Press, Inc., N.Y.

Redbook for "If she hadn't been there," by Marlo Thomas. From the February, 1977 issue of Redbook. All rights reserved. Reprinted by permission.

Donna Elker for "Mom." Copyright © Donna Elker, 1978. All rights reserved. Reprinted by permission.

Chandos Productions for "It seems God moves about her," by Joan Baez. From the book DAYBREAK, by Joan Baez. Copyright © 1966, 1968 by Joan Baez. All rights reserved. Reprinted by permission.

McCall Publishing Company for "She is just," by Rosalynn Carter. From the April, 1977 issue of McCall's. All rights reserved. Reprinted by permission.

Daniel Haughian for "Mothers." Copyright © Daniel Haughian, 1979. All rights reserved. Reprinted by permission.

Harper & Row, Publishers, Inc. for "I search among the plain," by Grace Noll Crowell. From the book LIGHT OF THE YEARS by Grace Noll Crowell. Copyright © 1936 by Harper & Row, Publishers, Inc.; renewed 1964 by Grace Noll Crowell. All rights reserved. Reprinted by permission.

Velvet Apple Music for "Forever is the love," by Dolly Parton. From the song SAY FOREVER YOU'LL BE MINE, by Dolly Parton. Copyright © 1971 by Owepar Publishing Co. All rights reserved. Reprinted by permission.

John Schaffner for "I have never met," by Edna St. Vincent Millay. From the book LETTERS OF EDNA ST. VINCENT MILLAY, edited by Allan Ross Macdougall. Published by Harper and Brothers, Copyright © 1952 by Norma Millay Ellis. Copyright © 1952 by Allan Ross Macdougall. All rights reserved. Reprinted by permission.

Lyle Stuart, Inc. for "Every thing in nature," by Kahlil Gibran. From the book A THIRD TREASURY OF KAHLIL GIBRAN edited by Andrew Dib Sherfan. Copyright © 1975, 1973, 1966, 1965 by Philosophical Library, Inc. All rights reserved. Reprinted by permission.

Edith Schaffer Lederberg for "Mothers are the daughters," by Edith Schaffer Lederberg. Copyright © 1979 by Edith Schaffer Lederberg. All rights reserved. Reprinted by permission.

Sue Mitchell for "Many joys," by Sue Mitchell. Copyright © 1980 by Sue Mitchell. All rights reserved. Reprinted by permission.

Jean Therese Lynch for "A Mother's Heart," by Jean Therese Lynch. Copyright © 1980 by Jean Therese Lynch. All rights reserved. Reprinted by permission.

Starboard Publishing Company for "Throughout our lives," by James Bruce Joseph Sievers. Copyright © 1976 by Starboard Publishing Company. All rights reserved. Reprinted by permission.

Diane Westlake for "total filling and flooding," by diane westlake. Copyright © Diane Westlake, 1980. All rights reserved. Reprinted by permission.

GALATIANS

The Wondrous Grace of God

JOHN MACARTHUR

THOMAS NELSON
Since 1798

GALATIANS
MACARTHUR BIBLE STUDIES

© 2007, John F. MacArthur, Jr.

Published in Nashville, Tennessee, by Nelson Books, an imprint of Thomas Nelson. Nelson Books and Thomas Nelson are registered trademarks of HarperCollins Christian Publishing, Inc.

Nelson Books titles may be purchased in bulk for education, business, fundraising, or sales promotional use. For information, please email SpecialMarkets@ThomasNelson.com

Published in association with the literary agency of Wolgemuth & Associates, Inc.

Produced with the assistance of the Livingstone Corporation. Project staff include Jake Barton, Betsy Todt Schmitt, and Andy Culbertson. Project editors: Mary Horner Collins, Amber Rae, and Len Woods

Scripture quotations marked NKJV are taken from the The New King James Version®. © 1982 by Thomas Nelson, Inc. Used by permission. All rights reserved.

"Unleashing God's Truth, One Verse at a Time" is a trademark of Grace to You. All rights reserved.

"Truth for Today" material is from *Galatians: MacArthur New Testament Commentary* (Moody Press: Chicago, IL, 1995) and from *The Glory of Heaven* by John MacArthur (Crossway Books: Wheaton, IL, 1996).

"Keys to the Text" material taken from the following sources:

Galatians: MacArthur New Testament Commentary (Moody Press: Chicago, IL, 1995). Used by permission. All rights reserved.

The MacArthur Study Bible (electronic ed.). John MacArthur, General Editor. © 1997 by Word Publishing. All rights reserved. Used by permission.

Nelson's New Illustrated Bible Dictionary, Rev. ed. R. F. Youngblood, F. F. Bruce, R. K. Harrison, editors. © 1995 by Thomas Nelson Publishers. Used by permission.

Romans: MacArthur New Testament Commentary Series (Moody Press: Chicago, IL, 1994). Used by permission.

Truth for Today: A Daily Touch of God's Grace by John MacArthur (J. Countryman: Nashville, TN, 2001).

Cover Art by Holly Sharp Design
Interior Design and Composition by Joel Bartlett, Livingstone Corporation

ISBN: 978-0-7180-3509-9

Printed in the United States of America.

HB 07.17.2017

CONTENTS

INTRODUCTION TO GALATIANS

Galatians derives its title *(pros Galatas)* from the region in Asia Minor (modern Turkey) where the churches addressed were located. This is Paul's only epistle specifically addressed to churches in more than one city (1:2; see 3:1; 1 Cor. 16:1).

AUTHOR AND DATE

There is no reason to question the internal claims that the apostle Paul wrote Galatians (1:1; 5:2). Paul was born in Tarsus, a city in the province of Cilicia, not far from Galatia. Under the famous rabbi Gamaliel, Paul received a thorough training in the Old Testament Scriptures and in the rabbinic traditions at Jerusalem (Acts 22:3). A member of the ultra-orthodox sect of the Pharisees (Acts 23:6), he was one of first-century Judaism's rising stars (1:14; see Phil. 3:5–6).

The course of Paul's life took a sudden and startling turn when, on his way to Damascus from Jerusalem to persecute Christians, he was confronted by the risen, glorified Christ (see Acts 9). That dramatic encounter turned Paul from Christianity's chief persecutor to its greatest missionary. His three missionary journeys and his trip to Rome turned Christianity from a faith that included only a small group of Palestinian Jewish believers into an empire-wide phenomenon. Galatians is one of thirteen inspired letters that Paul addressed to Gentile congregations or his fellow workers.

Chapter 2 describes Paul's visit to the Jerusalem Council of Acts 15 (see 2:1), so he must have written Galatians after that event. Since most scholars date the Jerusalem Council at about AD 49, the most likely date for Galatians is shortly thereafter.

BACKGROUND AND SETTING

In Paul's day, the word *Galatia* had two distinct meanings. In a strict ethnic sense, Galatia was the region of central Asia Minor inhabited by the Galatians. They were a Celtic people who had migrated to that region from Gaul (modern France) in the third century BC The Romans conquered the Galatians in 189 BC but allowed them to have some measure of independence until 25 BC, when Galatia became a Roman province, incorporating some regions not inhabited by ethnic Galatians (for example, parts of Lycaonia, Phrygia, and Pisidia). In a political sense, Galatia came to describe the entire Roman province, not merely the region inhabited by the ethnic Galatians.

Paul founded churches in the southern Galatian cities of Antioch, Iconium, Lystra, and Derbe (Acts 13:14–14:23). These cities, although within the Roman province of Galatia, were not in the ethnic Galatian region. There is no record of Paul's founding churches in that northern, less populated region.

Those two uses of the word Galatia make it more difficult to determine who the original recipients of the epistle were. Some interpret Galatia in its strict racial sense and argue that Paul addressed this epistle to churches in the northern Galatian region, inhabited by the ethnic descendants of the Gauls. Although the apostle apparently crossed the border into the fringes of ethnic Galatia on at least two occasions (Acts 16:6; 18:23), Acts does not record that he founded any churches or engaged in any evangelistic ministry there.

Because neither Acts nor Galatians mentions any cities or people from northern (ethnic) Galatia, it is reasonable to believe that Paul addressed this epistle to churches located in the southern part of the Roman province, but outside of the ethnic Galatian region. Acts records the apostle's founding of such churches at Pisidian Antioch (Acts 13:14–50), Iconium (Acts 13:51–14:7; see 16:2), Lystra (Acts 14:8–19; see 16:2), and Derbe (Acts 14:20–21; see 16:1). In addition, the churches Paul addressed had apparently been established before the Jerusalem Council (Gal. 2:5), and the churches of southern Galatia fit that criterion, having been founded during Paul's first missionary journey before the Council met. Paul did not visit northern (ethnic) Galatia until after the Jerusalem Council (Acts 16:6).

Paul wrote Galatians to counter Judaizing false teachers who were undermining the central New Testament doctrine of justification by faith (see Rom. 3:24). Ignoring the express decree of the Jerusalem Council (Acts 15:23–29), they were spreading a dangerous teaching that Gentiles must first become Jewish proselytes and submit to all the Mosaic Law before they could become Christians (Gal. 1:7; 4:17, 21; 5:2–12; 6:12–13). Shocked by the Galatians' openness to that damning heresy (1:6), Paul wrote this letter to defend justification by faith and warn these churches of the dire consequences of abandoning that essential doctrine. Galatians is Paul's only epistle that does not contain a commendation of its readers. This obvious omission reflects how urgently he felt about confronting the defection and defending the essential doctrine of justification.

Historical and Theological Themes

Galatians provides valuable historical information about Paul's background (chs. 1 and 2), that Acts does not mention; including his three-year stay in Nabatean Arabia (1:17–18), his fifteen-day visit with Peter after his stay in Arabia (1:18–19); his trip to the Jerusalem Council (2:1–10); and his confrontation of Peter (2:11–21).

As already noted, the central theme of Galatians (like that of Romans) is justification by faith. Paul defends that doctrine (the heart of the gospel) both in its theological (chs. 3 and 4) and practical (chs. 5 and 6) ramifications. Paul also defends his position as an apostle (chs. 1 and 2) since, as in Corinth, false teachers had attempted to gain a hearing for their heretical teaching by undermining his credibility. The main theological themes of Galatians are strikingly similar to those of Romans; for example, the inability of the law to justify (2:16; see Rom. 3:20); the believer's deadness to the law (Gal. 2:19; see Rom. 7:4); the believer's crucifixion with Christ (2:20; see Rom. 6:6); Abraham's justification by faith (3:6; see Rom. 4:3); believers as Abraham's spiritual children (3:7; see Rom. 4:10–11) and therefore blessed (3:9; see Rom. 4:23–24); the law bringing not salvation but God's wrath (3:10; see Rom. 4:15); the just living by faith (3:11; see Rom. 1:17); the universality of sin (3:22; see Rom. 11:32); believers as spiritually baptized into Christ (3:27; see Rom. 6:3); believers adopted as God's spiritual children (4:5–7; see Rom. 8:14–17); love fulfilling the law (5:14; see Rom. 13:8–10); the importance of walking in the Spirit (5:16; see Rom. 8:4); the warfare of the flesh against the Spirit (5:17; see Rom. 7:23, 25); the importance of believers bearing one another's burdens (6:2; see Rom. 15:1).

INTERPRETIVE CHALLENGES

First, Paul described a visit to Jerusalem and a subsequent meeting with Peter, James, and John (2:1–10). The text contains a question to be resolved, as to whether that was Paul's visit to the Jerusalem Council (Acts 15), or his earlier visit bringing famine relief to the Jerusalem church (Acts 11:27–30).

Second, those who teach baptismal regeneration (the false doctrine that baptism is necessary for salvation) support their view from Galatians 3:27.

Third, some have used this epistle to support their attacks on the biblical roles of men and women, claiming that the spiritual equality taught in 3:28 is incompatible with the traditional concept of authority and submission.

Fourth, those who reject the doctrine of eternal security argue that the phrase "you have fallen from grace" (5:4) describes believers who lost their salvation.

Fifth, there is disagreement whether Paul's statement, "See with what large letters I have written to you with my own hand!" refers to the entire letter or merely the concluding verses.

Finally, many claim that Paul erased the line between Israel and the church when he identified the church as the "Israel of God" (6:16).

_____

_____

_____

_____

_____

_____

_____

_____

_____

_____

_____

_____

_____

_____

_____

_____

_____

_____

_____

_____

_____

_____

_____

_____

_____

_____

_____

_____

DEPARTING FROM THE GOSPEL
Galatians 1:1–9

DRAWING NEAR

How and when did you first hear the good news of Jesus Christ? Explain.

_____

_____

_____

A common question asked by many evangelists when speaking to people about their spiritual condition is this: "Suppose you were to die today and found yourself standing before the heavenly gates. God Himself meets you there and asks, 'Why should I let you into heaven?' " What response would you give? What are some of the most common replies people give to this question?

_____

_____

_____

What would *you* say to that question? What do you think are the essentials of the gospel?

_____

_____

_____

THE CONTEXT

The gospel of Jesus Christ is good news to rebellious creatures facing the righteous judgment of a holy God. It is, in fact, the best news ever announced. The gospel liberates. It transforms. It saves.

This unearthly message of deliverance and hope changed the apostle Paul's life and radically redirected him. The transformation in Paul was so thorough that this former enemy of the gospel committed his life to traveling the known world to tell his marvelous story to anyone and everyone who would listen.

On his first missionary journey, Paul journeyed through Galatia (modern-day Turkey) preaching and establishing churches. Within a very short time, however, a number of prominent Jewish legalists (called Judaizers) infiltrated these grace communities and began teaching that faith in Christ alone was not enough to make a person right with God. Salvation, according to their convincing arguments, also required strict adherence to the Mosaic Law. The result was confused congregations and, ultimately, an angry apostle. Paul's deep concern over the churches' defection from the gospel is evident from the opening paragraphs of this letter, which lacks his customary commendations and courtesies and is, instead, brief and impersonal, with a sharp tone.

Is the purity of the gospel important? Is it all right to take an eclectic approach to spirituality—to mix elements of radically different faith traditions with the message of grace in Christ? Paul answers with a resounding "No!"

KEYS TO THE TEXT

Gospel: The Greek word translated as *gospel* means "a reward for bringing good news" or simply "good news." In His famous sermon at the synagogue in Nazareth, Jesus quoted Isaiah 61:1 to characterize the spirit of His ministry: "The Spirit of the LORD is upon Me, because He has anointed Me to preach the gospel [good news] to the poor" (Luke 4:18). The gospel does not reveal a new plan of salvation; it proclaims the fulfillment of God's plan of salvation that was begun in Israel, was completed in Jesus Christ, and is made known by the church. The gospel is the saving work of God in His Son Jesus Christ and a call to faith in Him. Jesus is more than a messenger of the gospel; He *is* the gospel. His life, teaching, and atoning death declared the good news of God. In turning from grace to a legalistic system of salvation by works, the Galatians had ignored the significance of the death of Christ. (*Nelson's New Illustrated Bible Dictionary*)

UNLEASHING THE TEXT

Read 1:1–9, noting the key words and definitions next to the passage.

apostle (v. 1)—In general terms, this word means "one who is sent with a commission." The apostles of Jesus Christ—the Twelve and Paul—were special ambassadors or messengers chosen and trained by Christ to lay the foundation of the early church and be the channels of God's completed revelation (Eph. 2:20).

Galatians 1:1–9 (NKJV)

1 *Paul, an apostle (not from men nor through man, but through Jesus Christ and God the Father who raised Him from the dead),*

not from men . . . but through Jesus Christ (v. 1)—To defend his apostleship against the false teachers' attack, Paul emphasized that Christ Himself had appointed him as an apostle before he met the other apostles (see vv. 17–18; Acts 9:3–9).

2 *and all the brethren who are with me, To the churches of Galatia:*

3 *Grace to you and peace from God the Father and our Lord Jesus Christ,*

4 *who gave Himself for our sins, that He might deliver us from this present evil age, according to the will of our God and Father,*

5 *to whom be glory forever and ever. Amen.*

6 *I marvel that you are turning away so soon from Him who called you in the grace of Christ, to a different gospel,*

7 *which is not another; but there are some who trouble you and want to pervert the gospel of Christ.*

raised Him from the dead (v. 1)—Paul included this important fact to show that the risen and ascended Christ Himself had appointed him; thus Paul was a qualified witness of Christ's resurrection (see Acts 1:22).

churches of Galatia (v. 2)—the churches Paul founded at Antioch of Pisidia, Iconium, Lystra, and Derbe during his first missionary journey (Acts 13:14–14:23)

Grace to you and peace (v. 3)—Even Paul's typical greeting attacked the Judaizers' legalistic system; if salvation is by works as they claimed, it is not of "grace" and cannot result in "peace," since no one can be sure he or she has enough good works to be eternally secure.

for our sins (v. 4)—No one can avoid sin by human effort or law-keeping (Rom. 3:20); therefore it must be forgiven, which Christ accomplished through His atoning death on the cross (Gal. 3:13).

present evil age (v. 4)—The Greek word for "age" does not refer to a period of time but an order or system and, in particular, to the current world system ruled by Satan (Rom. 12:2; 1 John 2:15–16; 5:19).

the will of our God (v. 4)—The sacrifice of Christ for salvation was the will of God designed and fulfilled for His glory (see Matt. 26:42; John 6:38–40).

turning away (v. 6)—This is better translated "deserting." The Greek word was used of military desertion which was punishable by death. The form of this Greek verb indicates that the Galatian believers were voluntarily deserting grace to pursue the legalism taught by the false teachers.

so soon (v. 6)—This Greek word can mean either "easily" or "quickly" and sometimes both. No doubt both senses characterized the Galatians' response to the false teachers' heretical doctrines.

called you (v. 6)—This could be translated "who called you once and for all" and refers to God's effectual call to salvation.

grace of Christ (v. 6)—God's free and sovereign act of mercy in granting salvation through the death and resurrection of Christ, totally apart from any human work or merit

different gospel (v. 6)—the Judaizers' perversion of the true gospel; they added the requirements, ceremonies, and standards of the old covenant as necessary prerequisites to salvation.

trouble (v. 7)—The Greek word could be translated "disturb" and means "to shake back and forth," meaning to agitate or stir up. Here it refers to the deep emotional disturbance that the Galatian believers experienced.

pervert (v. 7)—to turn something into its opposite. By adding law to the gospel of Christ, the false teachers were effectively destroying grace, turning the message of God's undeserved favor toward sinners into a message of earned and merited favor.

the gospel of Christ (v. 7)—the good news of salvation by grace alone through faith alone in Christ alone (Rom. 1:1; 1 Cor. 15:1–4)

we, or an angel from heaven (v. 8)—Paul's point is hypothetical, calling on the most unlikely examples for false teaching—himself and holy angels. The Galatians should receive no messenger, regardless of how impeccable his credentials, if his doctrine of salvation differs in the slightest degree from God's truth revealed through Christ and the apostles.

8 But even if we, or an angel from heaven, preach any other gospel to you than what we have preached to you, let him be accursed.

9 As we have said before, so now I say again, if anyone preaches any other gospel to you than what you have received, let him be accursed.

let him be accursed (v. 8)—The translation of this Greek word refers to devoting someone to destruction in eternal hell (see Rom. 9:3; 1 Cor. 12:3; 16:22). Throughout history, God has devoted certain objects, individuals, and groups of people to destruction (see Josh. 6:17–18; 7:1, 25–26). The New Testament offers many examples of one such group: false teachers (see Matt. 24:24; John 8:44; 1 Tim. 1:20; Titus 1:16). Here the Judaizers are identified as members of this infamous company.

As we have said before (v. 9)—This refers to what Paul taught during an earlier visit to these churches, not to a previous comment in this epistle.

anyone (v. 9)—Paul turns from the hypothetical case of verse 8 (the apostle or heavenly angels preaching a false gospel) to the real situation faced by the Galatians. The Judaizers were doing just that and were to be devoted to destruction because of their damning heresy.

1) How did Paul defend his apostleship? What was his primary argument?

directly sent commssioned by Jesus. No other credentials

(Verses to consider: Acts 9:1–15)

2) What was Paul's history with "the churches of Galatia"?

church founder. Original in establishing.

(Verses to consider: Acts 13:14–14:23)

3) According to Paul, what is the one and only solution for the problem of our sin?

Not justified by works but only faith.

(Verses to consider: Gal. 2:16; Eph. 2:8–9)

4) What did the death of Christ have to do with the will of God?

It was God's predermined plan. Law could not do. Christ as a sacrifice for sin.

(Verses to consider: *Acts 2:22–23; Rom. 8:3–4, 31–32; Eph. 1:7, 11; Heb. 10:4–10*)

Going Deeper

In Paul's letter to the church at Rome, he expounds on many of the same theological issues as in Galatians. Read Romans 3:19–28 for more insight about works and grace.

Romans 3:19–28 (NKJV)

19 *Now we know that whatever the law says, it says to those who are under the law, that every mouth may be stopped, and all the world may become guilty before God.*

20 *Therefore by the deeds of the law no flesh will be justified in His sight, for by the law is the knowledge of sin.*

21 *But now the righteousness of God apart from the law is revealed, being witnessed by the Law and the Prophets,*

22 *even the righteousness of God, through faith in Jesus Christ, to all and on all who believe. For there is no difference;*

23 *for all have sinned and fall short of the glory of God,*

24 *being justified freely by His grace through the redemption that is in Christ Jesus,*

25 *whom God set forth as a propitiation by His blood, through faith, to demonstrate His righteousness, because in His forbearance God had passed over the sins that were previously committed,*

26 *to demonstrate at the present time His righteousness, that He might be just and the justifier of the one who has faith in Jesus.*

27 *Where is boasting then? It is excluded. By what law? Of works? No, but by the law of faith.*

28 *Therefore we conclude that a man is justified by faith apart from the deeds of the law.*

Exploring the Meaning

5) How does the Romans 3 passage address the same problem facing the believers in Galatia?

Law or works are irrelevant for salvation, saved by faith

6) Read 2 Thessalonians 2:13–14. What does this say about the "call of God"? Why is this concept important for those who are tempted to turn away from grace and trust in works?

- God chose us through sanctification
- Saved by faith

(Verses to consider: 2 Tim. 1:8–9)

7) Read 2 Corinthians 11:3–4. What did Paul mean by a "different gospel"?

- Different gospel is not as "simple" we focus on todo not faith.
- Easily led away by activities we can complete

(Verses to consider: Gal. 3:3; 4:9)

Truth for Today

The most destructive dangers to the church have never been atheism, pagan religions, or cults that openly deny Scripture, but rather supposedly Christian movements that accept so much biblical truth that their unscriptural doctrines seem relatively insignificant and harmless. But a single drop of poison in a large container can make all the water lethal. And a single false idea that in any way undercuts God's grace poisons the whole system of belief.

REFLECTING ON THE TEXT

8) What is the simple gospel? Why do so many people find it hard to accept this?

- we are saved by faith.
- Too simple to fathom / understand.

9) Why do you think Paul reacted so harshly to the message of the Judaizers?

- He understood their motives and he knew the power of their deception

10) What is the danger of mixing grace with works?

Good Question.

11) List some relatives, friends, or neighbors who need to embrace the gospel of grace. Pray for them this week, asking God for the opportunity to speak with them about the good news of forgiveness and freedom in Christ.

- Myself. - Need to personally embrace grace and avoid sin.

PERSONAL RESPONSE

Write out additional reflections, questions you may have, or a prayer.

Lord help me to seek your grace through faith and avoid sin.

ADDITIONAL NOTES

2

DEFENDING THE GOSPEL
Galatians 1:10–2:10

DRAWING NEAR

In this section, the apostle Paul defends his credentials in order to prove the authority and authenticity of his message. In what ways do you think credentials are important?

_____

_____

_____

In what settings do you view a person's credentials as irrelevant?

_____

_____

_____

THE CONTEXT

After establishing churches in the region of Galatia on his first missionary journey, Paul learned that his work there was being undermined by a group commonly identified as the Judaizers. These Jewish loyalists were fiercely devoted to Mosaic ceremonies, standards, and practices and felt that Paul's gospel message was too far removed from its Jewish roots. They also argued that Paul's teaching was too easy and did not properly require enough demands of its adherents.

The Judaizers' response to this troublemaker named Paul was to try and thoroughly discredit him by attacking his credentials as an "apostle" of Christ. The strategy worked. Some Galatian believers began to question Paul's authority and legitimacy. Furthermore they questioned his motives. Most important, they began to doubt his message.

For all those reasons, Paul set out to defend his apostleship (1:10–2:10), explaining that he had been appointed by God and not by human beings. He offered a brief biographical sketch of important events in his life to further defend his calling and prove the authenticity of the gospel of grace he proclaimed. Then by recounting the details of his most significant trip to Jerusalem after his conversion, Paul offered convincing evidence that the message he proclaimed was identical to that of the other twelve apostles. By his coming, his companions, his commission, and his commendation, Paul powerfully demonstrated that he was of one truth and one spirit with the other twelve apostles. His gospel was independent in terms of revelation but identical in terms of content.

Paul's concern was not his own popularity or personal success, but God's truth. At stake was the very integrity of the gospel.

KEYS TO THE TEXT

Apostle: "One who is sent with a commission." An apostle was chosen and trained by Jesus Christ to proclaim His truth during the formative years of the church. In its primary usage, the term applied to the original twelve disciples chosen by Jesus at the beginning of His earthly ministry to lay the foundation of the early church. Jesus also gave them the power to perform healings and to cast out demons as verifying signs of their divine authority. Because Paul was not among the original twelve, he needed to defend his apostleship. One of the qualifications was witnessing the risen Christ (Acts 1:22). Paul explained to the Corinthian church that between His resurrection and ascension Jesus "was seen by Cephas [Peter], then by the twelve. . . . After that He was seen by James, then by all the apostles. Then last of all He was seen by me also" (1 Cor. 15:5–8). Paul witnessed the resurrected Christ in a unique way as he traveled to Damascus to arrest Christians there (Acts 9). Further personal appearances of the Lord to Paul are recorded in Acts 18:9; 22:17–21; 23:11; and 2 Corinthians 12:1–4.

UNLEASHING THE TEXT

Read 1:10–2:10, noting the key words and definitions next to the passage.

Galatians 1:10–2:10 (NKJV)

still pleased men (v. 10)—Paul's previous motivation when he used to persecute Christians on behalf of his fellow Jews

a bondservant of Christ (v. 10)—Paul had become a willing slave of Christ, which cost him a great deal of suffering from others (6:17). Such personal sacrifice is exactly opposite the goal of pleasing men (6:12).

10 *For do I now persuade men, or God? Or do I seek to please men? For if I still pleased men, I would not be a bondservant of Christ.*

11 *But I make known to you, brethren, that the gospel which was preached by me is not according to man.*

make known to you (v. 11)—The strong Greek verb used here would often introduce an important and emphatic statement (see 1 Cor. 12:3).

the gospel . . . not according to man (v. 11)—The gospel Paul preached was not human in origin or it would have been like all other human religions, permeated with "works righteousness"—earning salvation by good works—born of human pride and Satan's deception.

12 For I neither received it from man, nor was I taught it, but it came through the revelation of Jesus Christ.

13 For you have heard of my former conduct in Judaism, how I persecuted the church of God beyond measure and tried to destroy it.

14 And I advanced in Judaism beyond many of my contemporaries in my own nation, being more exceedingly zealous for the traditions of my fathers.

15 But when it pleased God, who separated me from my mother's womb and called me through His grace,

16 to reveal His Son in me, that I might preach Him among the Gentiles, I did not immediately confer with flesh and blood,

17 nor did I go up to Jerusalem to those who were apostles before me; but I went to Arabia, and returned again to Damascus.

neither received it from man, nor was I taught it (v. 12)—This is in contrast to the Judaizers, who received their religious instruction from rabbinic tradition. Most Jews did not study the actual Scriptures; instead, they used human interpretations of Scripture as their religious authority and guide. Many of their traditions were not only not taught in Scripture, but also contradicted it.

through the revelation (v. 12)—This refers to the unveiling of something previously kept secret—in this case, Jesus Christ. While he knew about Christ, Paul subsequently met Him personally on the road to Damascus and received the truth of the gospel from Him (Acts 9:1–16).

Judaism (v. 13)—the Jewish religious system of works righteousness, based not primarily on the Old Testament text but on rabbinic interpretations and traditions; in fact, Paul will argue that a proper understanding of the Old Testament can lead only to Christ and His gospel of grace through faith (Gal. 3:6–29).

persecuted (v. 13)—The tense of this Greek verb emphasizes Paul's persistent and continual effort to hurt and ultimately exterminate Christians.

advanced . . . beyond (v. 14)—The Greek word for "advanced" means "to chop ahead," much like one would blaze a trail through a forest. Paul blazed his path in Judaism (see Phil. 3:5–6), and because he saw Jewish Christians as obstacles to its advancement, he worked to cut them down.

exceedingly zealous (v. 14)—Paul demonstrated this by the extent to which he pursued and persecuted Christians.

traditions of my fathers (v. 14)—the oral teachings about Old Testament law commonly known as the "Halakah." This collection of interpretations of the law eventually carried the same authority as, or even greater than, the law (Torah) itself; its regulations were so hopelessly complex and burdensome that even the most astute rabbinical scholars could not master it by either interpretation or conduct.

separated me from my mother's womb (v. 15)—Paul is not talking about being born, separated physically from his mother but being separated or set apart to God for service from the time of his birth. The phrase refers to God's election of Paul without regard for his personal merit or effort (see Isa. 49:1).

called me through His grace (v. 15)—This refers to God's effectual call. On the Damascus Road God actually brought Saul, whom He had already chosen, to salvation.

reveal His Son in me (v. 16)—Not only was Christ revealed to Paul on the Damascus Road, but in him as God gave him the life, light, and faith to believe in Him.

preach Him among the Gentiles (v. 16)—Paul's specific call to proclaim the gospel to non-Jews

confer with flesh and blood (v. 16)—Paul did not look to Ananias or other Christians at Damascus for clarification of or addition to the revelation he received from Christ (Acts 9:19–20).

Jerusalem . . . Arabia . . . Damascus (v. 17)—Rather than immediately travel to Jerusalem to be instructed by the apostles, Paul instead went to Nabatean Arabia, a wilderness that stretched east of Damascus down to the Sinai peninsula. After being prepared for ministry by the Lord, he returned to minister in nearby Damascus.

three years (v. 18)—the approximate time from Paul's conversion to his first journey to Jerusalem. During those years he made a visit to Damascus and resided in Arabia, under the instruction of the Lord; this visit is discussed in Acts 9:26–30.

up to Jerusalem (v. 18)—Travelers in Israel always speak of going up to Jerusalem because of its higher elevation.

see (v. 18)—better translated "to become acquainted with"

Peter (v. 18)—the apostle who was the personal companion of the Lord and the most powerful spokesman in the early years of the Jerusalem church (Acts 1–12)

I do not lie (v. 20)—The directness of this statement indicates that Paul had been accused by the Jewish legalists of being a liar who was shameless or deluded.

18 *Then after three years I went up to Jerusalem to see Peter, and remained with him fifteen days.*

19 *But I saw none of the other apostles except James, the Lord's brother.*

20 *(Now concerning the things which I write to you, indeed, before God, I do not lie.)*

21 *Afterward I went into the regions of Syria and Cilicia.*

22 *And I was unknown by face to the churches of Judea which were in Christ.*

23 *But they were hearing only, "He who formerly persecuted us now preaches the faith which he once tried to destroy."*

24 *And they glorified God in me.*

2:1 *Then after fourteen years I went up again to Jerusalem with Barnabas, and also took Titus with me.*

2 *And I went up by revelation, and communicated to them that gospel which I preach among the Gentiles,*

Syria and Cilicia (v. 21)—This area included Paul's hometown of Tarsus—he preached in that region for several years. When word of revival in that area reached Jerusalem, they sent Barnabas (see Acts 11:20–26). Paul stayed in that region as a pastor in the church at Antioch. Then, with Barnabas, he went from there on the first missionary journey (Acts 13:1–3) and, afterward, returned to Antioch (Acts 13:1–3). From there they were sent to the Jerusalem Council (Acts 14:26–15:4).

fourteen years . . . again to Jerusalem (2:1)—This was the period from the time of his first visit to Jerusalem (Gal. 1:18) to the one to which Paul refers here, which probably was for the Jerusalem Council (Acts 15:1–22), called to resolve the issue of Gentile salvation. Linguistically, the word "again" need not refer to the next visit; it can just as easily mean "once again" without respect to how many visits took place in between. Paul did, in fact, visit Jerusalem during that fourteen-year period to deliver famine relief to the church there (Acts 11:27–30; 12:24–25), but he does not refer to that visit here since it had no bearing on his apostolic authority.

Barnabas (v. 1)—Paul's first ally who vouched for him before the apostles at Jerusalem (Acts 9:27) and who became Paul's traveling companion on his first missionary journey (Acts 13:2–3)

Titus (v. 1)—a spiritual child of Paul and a coworker (Titus 1:4–5); as an uncircumcised Gentile, Titus was fitting proof of the effectiveness of Paul's ministry.

by revelation (v. 2)—This revelation from God was the voice of the Holy Spirit. Paul referred to the divine commissioning of his visit in order to refute any suggestion by the Judaizers that they had sent Paul to Jerusalem to have the apostles correct his doctrine.

those who were of reputation (v. 2)—the three main leaders of the Jerusalem church: Peter, James (the Lord's brother, 1:19), and John (see v. 9). This phrase was typically used of authorities and implied a position of honor. Paul referred to them in a similar way two other times (vv. 6, 9), suggesting a hint of sarcasm directed toward the Judaizers, who claimed they had apostolic approval for their doctrine and Paul did not; they had likely made a habit of exalting these three leaders at Paul's expense.

but privately to those who were of reputation, lest by any means I might run, or had run, in vain.

3 *Yet not even Titus who was with me, being a Greek, was compelled to be circumcised.*

4 *And this occurred because of false brethren secretly brought in (who came in by stealth to spy out our liberty which we have in Christ Jesus, that they might bring us into bondage),*

5 *to whom we did not yield submission even for an hour, that the truth of the gospel might continue with you.*

6 *But from those who seemed to be something— whatever they were, it makes no difference to me; God shows personal favoritism to no man—for those who seemed to be something added nothing to me.*

7 *But on the contrary, when they saw that the gospel for the uncircumcised had been committed to me, as the gospel for the circumcised was to Peter*

8 *(for He who worked effectively in Peter for the apostleship to the circumcised also worked effectively in me toward the Gentiles),*

might run . . . in vain (v. 2)—Paul hoped the Jerusalem leaders would support his ministry to the Gentiles and not soften their opposition to legalism. He did not want to see his ministry efforts wasted because of conflict with the other apostles.

compelled to be circumcised (v. 3)—At the core of the Judaizers' works system was the Mosaic prescription of circumcision. They were teaching that there could be no salvation without circumcision (Acts 15:1, 5, 24). Paul and the apostles denied that assertion, and it was settled at the Jerusalem Council. As a true believer, Titus was living proof that circumcision and the Mosaic regulations were not prerequisites or necessary components of salvation. The apostles' refusal to require Titus's circumcision verified the church's rejection of the Judaizers' doctrine.

false brethren (v. 4)—the Judaizers, who pretended to be true Christians; yet their doctrine, because it claimed allegiance to Christ, was opposed to traditional Judaism, and, because it demanded circumcision and obedience to the Mosaic Law as prerequisites for salvation, was opposed to Christianity.

to spy out (v. 4)—The Greek word pictures spies or traitors entering by stealth into an enemy's camp. The Judaizers were Satan's undercover agents sent into the midst of the church to sabotage the true gospel.

liberty (v. 4)—Christians are free from the law as a means of salvation, from its external ceremonial regulations as a way of living, and from its curse for disobedience to the law—a curse that Christ bore for all believers (3:13). This freedom is not, however, a license to sin (5:13).

bondage (v. 4)—conveys the idea of absolute slavery to an impossible system of works righteousness

those who seemed to be something (v. 6)—another reference to Peter, James, and John

personal favoritism (v. 6)—The unique privileges of the Twelve did not make their apostleship more legitimate or authoritative than Paul's—Christ commissioned them all (see Rom. 2:11). Paul never saw himself as apostolically inferior.

for the uncircumcised (v. 7)—better translated "to the uncircumcised"; Paul preached the gospel primarily to the Gentiles (also to Jews in Gentile lands, as his pattern was to go to the synagogue first; see Acts 13:5).

circumcised . . . Peter (v. 7)—Peter's ministry was primarily to the Jews.

He who worked effectively in Peter . . . in me (v. 8)—The Holy Spirit, who has but one gospel, empowered both Peter and Paul in their ministries.

pillars (v. 9)—emphasizing the role of James, Peter, and John in establishing and supporting the church

the right hand of fellowship (v. 9)—In the Near East, this represented a solemn vow of friendship and a mark of partnership. This act signified the apostles' recognition of Paul as a teacher of the true gospel and a partner in ministry.

9 and when James, Cephas, and John, who seemed to be pillars, perceived the grace that had been given to me, they gave me and Barnabas the right hand of fellowship, that we should go to the Gentiles and they to the circumcised.

10 They desired only that we should remember the poor, the very thing which I also was eager to do.

remember the poor (v. 10)—a practical reminder for Paul and the growing ranks of Gentile Christians; the number of Christians in Jerusalem grew rapidly at first (see Acts 2:41–45; 6:1), and many who were visiting the city for the feast of Pentecost (Acts 2:1, 5) remained and never returned to their homes; while the believers initially shared their resources (Acts 2:45; 4:32–37), many had little money, and for years the Jerusalem church was economically pressed.

1) What does Paul reveal as the driving force behind his actions in the past? How does that compare with his current motivation?

_____

_____

_____

_____

2) How does Paul's conversion demonstrate the truth of election and give authority to his ministry?

_____

_____

_____

(Verse to consider: Jer. 1:5)

3) Where and how did Paul receive his initial preparation for ministry?

_____

_____

_____

_____

4) When Paul eventually conferred with the other apostles, how did they react to his message and his ministry among the Gentiles? How does this contribute to the argument Paul is making about the authenticity of his message?

_____

_____

_____

GOING DEEPER

Read Philippians 3:1–14 for more insight into the dangers of legalism.

Philippians 3:1–14 (NKJV)

1 *Finally, my brethren, rejoice in the Lord. For me to write the same things to you is not tedious, but for you it is safe.*

2 *Beware of dogs, beware of evil workers, beware of the mutilation!*

3 *For we are the circumcision, who worship God in the Spirit, rejoice in Christ Jesus, and have no confidence in the flesh,*

4 *though I also might have confidence in the flesh. If anyone else thinks he may have confidence in the flesh, I more so:*

5 *circumcised the eighth day, of the stock of Israel, of the tribe of Benjamin, a Hebrew of the Hebrews; concerning the law, a Pharisee;*

6 *concerning zeal, persecuting the church; concerning the righteousness which is in the law, blameless.*

7 *But what things were gain to me, these I have counted loss for Christ.*

8 *Yet indeed I also count all things loss for the excellence of the knowledge of Christ Jesus my Lord, for whom I have suffered the loss of all things, and count them as rubbish, that I may gain Christ*

9 *and be found in Him, not having my own righteousness, which is from the law, but that which is through faith in Christ, the righteousness which is from God by faith;*

10 *that I may know Him and the power of His resurrection, and the fellowship of His sufferings, being conformed to His death,*

11 *if, by any means, I may attain to the resurrection from the dead.*

12 *Not that I have already attained, or am already perfected; but I press on, that I may lay hold of that for which Christ Jesus has also laid hold of me.*

13 *Brethren, I do not count myself to have apprehended; but one thing I do, forgetting those things which are behind and reaching forward to those things which are ahead,*

14 *I press toward the goal for the prize of the upward call of God in Christ Jesus.*

Exploring the Meaning

5) What is Paul's attitude toward his religious "credentials"?

_____

_____

_____

6) How does Paul's testimony in Philippians 3 corroborate his statements in Galatians 1:10–2:10?

_____

_____

_____

7) Read Genesis 17:9–14. What was the point of circumcision for the Jews?

_____

_____

_____

(Verses to consider: Rom. 4:9–12)

8) Read Acts 15:1–22. How did the events and decisions of the Jerusalem Council give credence to Paul's apostolic claims?

_____

_____

_____

Truth for Today

No human explanation or influence could account for the 180-degree turn-around in Saul's life. He had been like a runaway freight train that crushes everything in its path. He had lost control of his life and was without restraint. His legalistic zeal had put him on a headlong course of destruction from which no natural force short of death could have deterred him. His apostolic calling could only have been supernatural and sovereign, completely apart from human testimony or persuasion (though he may have heard much truth from the Christians he captured).

REFLECTING ON THE TEXT

9) If a group of religious people attacked your character and motives and accused you of propagating a suspect faith, how would you answer them? What evidence would you marshal to establish your authenticity as a servant of the Lord Jesus Christ?

_____

_____

_____

_____

10) Like Paul, most ministers face a pretty steady barrage of accusations and unwarranted attacks. How can you (concretely and practically) offer encouragement to your pastor today?

_____

_____

_____

_____

11) Identify at least three areas where your actions are motivated primarily by the desire to please other people. What would change if pleasing God became your sole motivation?

_____

_____

_____

_____

12) Which of your credentials ultimately matters the most? How can you better use your gifts, experiences, and training to serve the Lord more effectively this week?

_____

_____

_____

_____

Personal Response

Write out additional reflections, questions you may have, or a prayer.

_____

_____

_____

_____

_____

_____

_____

_____

_____

_____

_____

_____

_____

_____

_____

_____

_____

_____

_____

_____

_____

_____

_____

_____

_____

_____

3

CRUCIFIED WITH CHRIST
Galatians 2:11–21

DRAWING NEAR

Paul had no problem confronting people who distorted the truth of the gospel. Our society's current emphasis on "tolerance" contributes to the rarity of confronting others with truth. How is this dangerous?

_____

_____

_____

What is it about human nature that balks at the notion of grace—God's unearned favor?

_____

_____

_____

THE CONTEXT

Early Christianity had a distinctively Jewish flavor. The early church began almost exclusively with converts from Jewish backgrounds and personal histories steeped in Hebrew traditions and practices. When large numbers of Gentiles also began embracing Jesus Christ as Messiah, the result was a collision of very radically different cultural and religious worlds.

In and around this strange and new entity called the church rose a group determined to cling to the old legalism of the Mosaic Law. These were the Judaizers—devout God-fearing people claiming to follow Christ but teaching that Gentiles must be circumcised and adhere to the Mosaic Law. Not only did these Judaizers distort the gospel and confuse the Gentile converts in Galatia, but they also called into question Paul's apostolic claims. In response, Paul wrote Galatians, a very stern and blunt letter about the good news of justification by faith.

In this section, Paul relates how he confronted Peter, the preeminent apostle, because of Peter's failure to live up to the truth of the gospel. Peter had withdrawn from the Gentile believers to fellowship with the Judaizers, although they held a position he knew was wrong. By so doing, Peter had in appearance supported their doctrine and had nullified Paul's divine teaching, especially the doctrine of salvation by grace alone through faith alone. Paul's rebuke of Peter serves as one of the most dynamic statements in the New Testament on the absolute and unwavering necessity of the doctrine of justification by grace through faith.

KEYS TO THE TEXT

Judaizers: Devout, God-fearing, Jewish religious leaders who attempted to add to the gospel the legalistic requirements of the Old Testament, such as circumcision and obedience to the Sabbath laws. The Judaizers who plagued the early church claimed to be Christians, and much of their doctrine was orthodox. They must have recognized Jesus as the promised Messiah and even acknowledged the value of His sacrificial death on the cross—otherwise they would never have gotten a hearing in the church. They claimed to believe all the truths that other Christians believed. They did not purport to overtly deny the gospel but to improve it by adding the requirements, ceremonies, and standards of the old covenant to the New. This spirit of legalism was carried into the church by many Jews who had taken on the name of Christ.

Grace: The only gospel of God is the gospel of grace, which is the gospel of divine redemption totally apart from any work or merit of man. "For by grace you have been saved through faith," Paul declared to the Ephesians, "and that not of yourselves, it is the gift of God; not as a result of works, that no one should boast. For we are His workmanship" (Eph. 2:8–10). And it is continually that "grace in which we stand" (Rom. 5:2). We live in grace from the moment of salvation, and if grace ever stopped, we would lose our undeserved salvation and perish in sin. The grace of Christ is God's free and sovereign act of love and mercy in granting salvation through the death and resurrection of Jesus, apart from anything men are or can do, and of His sustaining that salvation to glorification. It is absurd to accept a gracious salvation and then endeavor to maintain righteousness through human efforts, ceremonies, and ritual.

UNLEASHING THE TEXT

Read 2:11–21, noting the key words and definitions next to the passage.

Galatians 2:11–21 (NKJV)

11 Now when Peter had come to Antioch, I withstood him to his face, because he was to be blamed;

12 for before certain men came from James, he would eat with the Gentiles; but when they came, he withdrew and separated himself, fearing those who were of the circumcision.

13 And the rest of the Jews also played the hypocrite with him, so that even Barnabas was carried away with their hypocrisy.

14 But when I saw that they were not straightforward about the truth of the gospel, I said to Peter before them all, "If you, being a Jew, live in the manner of Gentiles and not as the Jews, why do you compel Gentiles to live as Jews?

15 "We who are Jews by nature, and not sinners of the Gentiles,

16 "knowing that a man is not justified by the works of the law but by faith in Jesus Christ, even we have

Antioch (v. 11)—the location of the first Gentile church

to be blamed (v. 11)—better translated "stood condemned"; Peter was guilty of sin by aligning himself with men he knew to be in error and because of the harm and confusion he caused his Gentile brethren.

certain men . . . from James (v. 12)—Peter, knowing the decision the Jerusalem Council had made (Acts 15:7–29), had been in Antioch for some time, eating with Gentiles. When Judaizers came, pretending to be sent by James, they lied, giving false claims of support from the apostles. Peter had already given up all Mosaic ceremony (Acts 10:9–22), and James had, at times, held only to some of it (Acts 21:18–26).

withdrew (v. 12)—The Greek term refers to strategic military withdrawal. The verb's form may imply that Peter's withdrawal was gradual and deceptive. To eat with the Judaizers and decline invitations to eat with the Gentiles, which he had previously done, meant that Peter was affirming the very dietary restrictions he knew God had abolished (Acts 10:15), and thus striking a blow at the gospel of grace.

fearing those . . . of the circumcision (v. 12)—The true motivation behind Peter's defection was that he was afraid of losing popularity with the legalistic, Judaizing segment of people in the church, even though they were self-righteous hypocrites promoting a heretical doctrine.

the rest of the Jews (v. 13)—the Jewish believers in Antioch

hypocrite (v. 13)—This Greek word refers to an actor who would wear a mask to depict a mood or certain character. In the spiritual sense, it refers to someone who masks his true character by pretending to be something he is not—they were committed to the gospel of grace but were pretending to accept Jewish legalism.

straightforward (v. 14)—literally, to walk "straight" or "uprightly." By withdrawing from the Gentile Christians, Peter and the other Jewish believers were not walking in line with God's Word.

live in the manner of Gentiles (v. 14)—Before his gradual withdrawal, Peter regularly had fellowship and ate with the Gentiles, thus modeling the ideal of Christian love and liberty between Jew and Gentile.

compel Gentiles to live as Jews (v. 14)—By his Judaizing mandate, Peter was declaring that theirs was the right way.

sinners of the Gentiles (v. 15)—This is used in the legal sense since Gentiles were sinners by nature because they had no revealed, divine, written law to guide them toward salvation or living righteously.

works . . . faith (v. 16)—Three times this verse declares that salvation is only through faith in Christ and not by law. The first is general, "a man is not justified"; the second is personal, "we might be justified"; and the third is universal, "no flesh shall be justified."

justified (v. 16)—This basic forensic Greek word describes a judge declaring an accused person not guilty and therefore innocent before the law. Throughout Scripture it refers to God's declaring a sinner not guilty and fully righteous before Him by imputing to him the divine righteousness of Christ and imputing the person's sin to the sinless Savior for punishment.

works of the law (v. 16)—Keeping the law is not a means of salvation because the root of sinfulness is in the fallenness of a person's heart, not his or her actions. The law served as a mirror to reveal sin, not a cure for it.

we . . . are found sinners (v. 17)—If the Judaizers' doctrine was correct, then Paul, Peter, Barnabas, and the other Jewish believers had fallen back into the category of sinners because they had been eating and fellowshiping with Gentiles, who, according to the Judaizers, were unclean.

believed in Christ Jesus, that we might be justified by faith in Christ and not by the works of the law; for by the works of the law no flesh shall be justified.

17 "But if, while we seek to be justified by Christ, we ourselves also are found sinners, is Christ therefore a minister of sin? Certainly not!

18 "For if I build again those things which I destroyed, I make myself a transgressor.

19 "For I through the law died to the law that I might live to God.

20 "I have been crucified with Christ; it is no longer I who live, but Christ lives in me; and the life which I now live in the flesh I live by faith in the Son of God, who loved me and gave Himself for me.

21 "I do not set aside the grace of God; for if righteousness comes through the law, then Christ died in vain."

minister of sin (v. 17)—If the Judaizers were right, then Christ was wrong and had been teaching people to sin because He taught that food could not contaminate a person. Jesus also had declared that all who belong to Him are one with Him and therefore each other (John 17:21–23). Paul's airtight logic condemned Peter because by his actions he had, in effect, made it appear as if Christ were lying. This thought is utterly objectionable and caused Paul to use the strongest Greek negative ("certainly not"; see 3:21; Rom. 6:1–2; 7:13).

things which I destroyed (v. 18)—the false system of salvation through legalism, done away with by the preaching of salvation by grace alone through faith alone

died to the law (v. 19)—When a person is convicted of a capital crime and executed, the law has no further claim on that person. So it is with the Christian who has died in Christ (who paid the penalty for his sins in full) and rises to new life in Him—justice has been satisfied and the believer is forever free from any further penalty.

I have been crucified with Christ (v. 20)—A person who trusts in Christ for salvation spiritually participates with the Lord in His crucifixion and victory over sin and death.

no longer I who live, but Christ lives in me (v. 20)—The believer's old self is dead, having been crucified with Christ (Rom. 6:3, 5). The believer's new person has the privilege of the indwelling Christ empowering him or her and living through him or her.

gave Himself for me (v. 20)—the manifestation of Christ's love for the believer through His sacrificial death on the cross

Christ died in vain (v. 21)—This can be better translated, "Christ died needlessly." Those who insist that they can earn salvation by their own efforts undermine the foundation of Christianity and render unnecessary the death of Christ.

1) How did Peter deviate from the true gospel and become hypocritical? How did Paul respond to this?

_____

_____

_____

_____

_____

_____

_____

(Verses to consider: Acts 10)

2) If the law is incapable of saving people, as Paul argued, what is the law's purpose?

_____

_____

_____

_____

_____

_____

_____

(Verses to consider: Rom. 7:7–13; Gal. 3:22–25; 1 Tim. 1:8–11)

3) How did Paul contrast the teaching of the Judaizers with the teaching of Christ?

_____

_____

_____

_____

_____

(Verses to consider: Mark 7:18–23; John 17:20–23; Acts 10:13–15)

4) According to 2:20–21, how does the believer's union with Christ refute the argument of the Judaizers and the wrong behavior of Peter?

_____

_____

_____

_____

_____

_____

Going Deeper

Paul confronted Peter about basic issues of salvation. To find out how God changed Peter's mind about Gentiles also being saved by grace, read Acts 11:1–18.

Acts 11:1–18 (NKJV)

1 *Now the apostles and brethren who were in Judea heard that the Gentiles had also received the word of God.*

2 *And when Peter came up to Jerusalem, those of the circumcision contended with him,*

3 *saying, "You went in to uncircumcised men and ate with them!"*

4 *But Peter explained it to them in order from the beginning, saying:*

5 *"I was in the city of Joppa praying; and in a trance I saw a vision, an object descending like a great sheet, let down from heaven by four corners; and it came to me.*

6 *"When I observed it intently and considered, I saw four-footed animals of the earth, wild beasts, creeping things, and birds of the air.*

7 *"And I heard a voice saying to me, 'Rise, Peter; kill and eat.'*

8 *"But I said, 'Not so, Lord! For nothing common or unclean has at any time entered my mouth.'*

9 *"But the voice answered me again from heaven, 'What God has cleansed you must not call common.'*

10 *"Now this was done three times, and all were drawn up again into heaven.*

11 *"At that very moment, three men stood before the house where I was, having been sent to me from Caesarea.*

12 *"Then the Spirit told me to go with them, doubting nothing. Moreover these six brethren accompanied me, and we entered the man's house.*

13 *"And he told us how he had seen an angel standing in his house, who said to him, 'Send men to Joppa, and call for Simon whose surname is Peter,*

14 *"who will tell you words by which you and all your household will be saved.'*

15 *"And as I began to speak, the Holy Spirit fell upon them, as upon us at the beginning.*

16 *"Then I remembered the word of the Lord, how He said, 'John indeed baptized with water, but you shall be baptized with the Holy Spirit.'*

17 *"If therefore God gave them the same gift as He gave us when we believed on the Lord Jesus Christ, who was I that I could withstand God?"*

18 *When they heard these things they became silent; and they glorified God, saying, "Then God has also granted to the Gentiles repentance to life."*

EXPLORING THE MEANING

5) What enabled Peter to stand up to the Judaizers' accusations of eating with uncircumcised Gentiles?

_____

_____

_____

_____

6) What role did the Holy Spirit play in spreading the gospel? What role did the Spirit play in Peter's life and growth?

_____

_____

_____

_____

7) Read Romans 6:2–6. How does this passage amplify Paul's statement in Galatians 2:20?

_____

_____

_____

_____

_____

(Verses to consider: Rom. 8:9–10; Eph. 4:22)

Truth for Today

The two pillars of the gospel are the grace of God and the death of Christ, and those are the two pillars that, by its very nature, legalism destroys. The person who insists that he can earn salvation by his own efforts undermines the very foundation of Christianity and nullifies the precious death of Christ on his behalf.

Reflecting on the Text

8) The Galatian believers were tempted to think that human effort of keeping Jewish laws and customs was essential to salvation. Modern-day Christians don't typically try to adhere to the Mosaic Law in an attempt to earn God's favor, but what kinds of "Christian laws" are often held up as necessary for meeting God's approval?

_____

_____

_____

_____

9) What does it mean to you to be "crucified with Christ"?

_____

_____

_____

_____

10) What truth or principle from this lesson has had the greatest impact on you personally? Why? What will you do differently as a result?

_____

_____

_____

_____

PERSONAL RESPONSE

Write out additional reflections, questions you may have, or a prayer.

Additional Notes

4

JUSTIFICATION BY FAITH
Galatians 3:1–9

DRAWING NEAR

Paul went to great lengths to help the early Christians stay faithful and not
lose sight of all that Christ had done for them. Have you experienced a
time in your Christian life when you were sidetracked by nonessentials or
deceived by false teaching? If so, explain what happened.

_____

_____

_____

How do you define "faith"?

_____

_____

_____

THE CONTEXT

Paul had introduced the gospel of sovereign grace to the Galatians, bringing them
the truth that salvation is received through faith in Christ's atoning work on the
cross plus nothing else. Now these believers were drifting and had accepted an
inferior and impotent substitute based on the old Mosaic rituals and ceremonial
standards that the new covenant in Christ had made invalid—and that, even
under the old covenant, had no power to save.

The defecting believers had not lost their salvation, but they had lost the joy
and freedom of it and had returned, deceived, to the uncertainty and bondage of
a self-imposed legalism. They were still in Christ and right with God positionally,
but they were not practically living in conformity to the truth by which they had
been made righteous. Having substituted a form of religion, they had no power
or joy for the fullness of life in Christ that they once enjoyed.

Because these believers had allowed themselves to be deceived, they also
were projecting to the deceived unbelievers around them the thinking that
Christianity was a matter of law rather than faith. They had robbed themselves
of the fullness of God's blessing and were in danger of robbing the world of the
knowledge of the only way of salvation.

In this passage, Paul reminds the Galatians that a believer's experience with the Lord Jesus Christ, with the Holy Spirit, and with God the Father is incontrovertible evidence of having been graciously made acceptable to God through personal faith in the perfect and complete work of Christ, apart from any human supplement. Paul uses Abraham as proof that salvation has never come any other way than by grace through faith. Even the Old Testament teaches justification by faith.

Keys to the Text

Justification: This legal term comes from the Greek word for "righteous" and means "to declare righteous." This verdict includes: pardon from the guilt and penalty of sin, as well as the imputation of Christ's righteousness to the believer's account, which provides for the positive righteousness man needs to be accepted by God. God declares a sinner righteous solely on the basis of the merits of Christ's righteousness. God imputes a believer's sin to Christ's account in His sacrificial death. The sinner receives this gift of God's grace by faith alone. Justification is a gracious gift God extends to the repentant, believing sinner—wholly apart from human merit or work.

Abraham: Paul uses the model of Abraham to prove justification by faith alone because the Jews held him up as the supreme example of a righteous man (John 8:39), and because it clearly showed that Judaism with its works-based righteousness had deviated from the faith of the Jews' patriarchal ancestors. In a spiritual sense, Abraham was the forerunner of the primarily Gentile church in Rome as well.

Unleashing the Text

Read 3:1–9, noting the key words and definitions next to the passage.

foolish (v. 1)—This refers not to lack of intelligence but to lack of obedience (see Luke 24:25; 1 Tim. 6:9). Paul expressed his shock, surprise, and outrage at the Galatians' defection by pointing out that "Jesus Christ was clearly portrayed among you as crucified."

Galatians 3:1–9 (NKJV)

1 *O foolish Galatians! Who has bewitched you that you should not obey the truth, before whose eyes Jesus Christ was clearly portrayed among you as crucified?*

Who . . . ? (v. 1)—The Judaizers, the Jewish false teachers, were plaguing the Galatian churches.

bewitched (v. 1)—charmed or misled by flattery and false promises; the term suggests an appeal to the emotions

2 *This only I want to learn from you: Did you receive the Spirit by the works of the law, or by the hearing of faith?—*

3 *Are you so foolish? Having begun in the Spirit, are you now being made perfect by the flesh?*

4 *Have you suffered so many things in vain—if indeed it was in vain?*

5 *Therefore He who supplies the Spirit to you and works miracles among you, does He do it by the works of the law, or by the hearing of faith?*

6 *just as Abraham "believed God, and it was accounted to him for righteousness."*

7 *Therefore know that only those who are of faith are sons of Abraham.*

8 *And the Scripture, foreseeing that God would justify the Gentiles by faith, preached the gospel to Abraham beforehand, saying, "In you all the nations shall be blessed."*

9 *So then those who are of faith are blessed with believing Abraham.*

clearly portrayed (v. 1)—The Greek word describes the posting of official notices in public places. Paul's preaching had publicly displayed the true gospel of Jesus Christ before the Galatians.

crucified (v. 1)—The crucifixion of Christ was a one-time historical fact with continuing results into eternity. Christ's sacrificial death provides eternal payment for believers' sins (see Heb. 7:25) and does not need to be supplemented by any human works.

Did you receive the Spirit. . . ? (v. 2)—The answer to Paul's rhetorical question is obvious; the Galatians had received the Spirit when they were saved (Rom. 8:9; 1 John 3:24), not through keeping the law, but through saving faith granted when hearing the gospel (see Rom. 10:17)—the hearing of faith is actually hearing with faith. Paul appealed to the Galatians' own salvation to refute the Judaizers' false teaching that keeping the law is necessary for salvation.

Are you so foolish? (v. 3)—Incredulous at how easily the Galatians had been duped, Paul asked a second rhetorical question, again rebuking them for their foolishness.

begun in the Spirit . . . by the flesh (v. 3)—The notion that sinful, weak, fallen human nature could improve on the saving work of the Holy Spirit was ludicrous to Paul.

suffered (v. 4)—The Greek word has the basic meaning of "experienced" and does not necessarily imply pain or hardship. Paul used it to describe the Galatians' personal experience of salvation in Jesus Christ.

many things (v. 4)—This refers to all the blessings of salvation from God, Christ, and the Holy Spirit (see Eph. 1:3).

sons of Abraham (v. 7)—quoted from Genesis 15:6; believing Jews and Gentiles are the true spiritual children of Abraham because they follow his example of faith (see Gal. 3:29; Rom. 4:11, 16).

Scripture, foreseeing (v. 8)—Personifying the Scriptures was a common Jewish figure of speech (see Gal. 4:30; John 7:38, 42; 19:37; Rom. 9:17; 11:2). Because Scripture is God's Word, when it speaks, God speaks.

preached the gospel to Abraham (v. 8)—The "good news" to Abraham was the news of salvation for all the nations (quoted from Gen. 12:3; 18:18—see Gen. 22:18; John 8:56; Acts 26:22–23). Salvation has always been by faith.

those who are of faith . . . Abraham (v 9)—whether Jew or Gentile; the Old Testament predicted that Gentiles would receive the blessings of justification by faith, as did Abraham; those blessings are poured out on all because of Christ (see John 1:16; Eph. 1:3; Col. 2:10; 2 Pet. 1:3–4)

1) Why did Paul describe the Galatians as "foolish" and "bewitched"?

_____

_____

_____

_____

_____

_____

(Verses to consider: Luke 24:25; Rom. 12:1, 2)

2) What did Paul say about the connection between the Holy Spirit and salvation? Specifically, when do believers receive the Spirit?

_____

_____

_____

_____

_____

_____

3) What evidence resulted in God's verdict declaring Abraham righteous? How would this undermine the Judaizers' argument?

_____

_____

_____

_____

_____

_____

4) Based on this passage, who qualifies to receive the same spiritual blessings as Abraham?

_____

_____

_____

_____

_____

_____

(Verses to consider: Rom. 8:32; Eph. 2:6–7)

GOING DEEPER

In a related passage, Paul expounds more on Abraham's saving faith. Read Romans 4:1–25.

Romans 4:1–25 (NKJV)

1 *What then shall we say that Abraham our father has found according to the flesh?*

2 *For if Abraham was justified by works, he has something to boast about, but not before God.*

3 *For what does the Scripture say? "Abraham believed God, and it was accounted to him for righteousness."*

4 *Now to him who works, the wages are not counted as grace but as debt.*

5 *But to him who does not work but believes on Him who justifies the ungodly, his faith is accounted for righteousness,*

6 *just as David also describes the blessedness of the man to whom God imputes righteousness apart from works:*

7 *"Blessed are those whose lawless deeds are forgiven, And whose sins are covered;*

8 *Blessed is the man to whom the LORD shall not impute sin."*

9 *Does this blessedness then come upon the circumcised only, or upon the uncircumcised also? For we say that faith was accounted to Abraham for righteousness.*

10 *How then was it accounted? While he was circumcised, or uncircumcised? Not while circumcised, but while uncircumcised.*

11 *And he received the sign of circumcision, a seal of the righteousness of the faith which he had while still uncircumcised, that he might be the father of all those who believe, though they are uncircumcised, that righteousness might be imputed to them also,*

12 *and the father of circumcision to those who not only are of the circumcision, but who also walk in the steps of the faith which our father Abraham had while still uncircumcised.*

13 *For the promise that he would be the heir of the world was not to Abraham or to his seed through the law, but through the righteousness of faith.*

14 *For if those who are of the law are heirs, faith is made void and the promise made of no effect,*

15 *because the law brings about wrath; for where there is no law there is no transgression.*

16 *Therefore it is of faith that it might be according to grace, so that the promise might be sure to all the seed, not only to those who are of the law, but also to those who are of the faith of Abraham, who is the father of us all*

17 *(as it is written, "I have made you a father of many nations") in the presence of Him whom he believed—God, who gives life to the dead and calls those things which do not exist as though they did;*

18 *who, contrary to hope, in hope believed, so that he became the father of many nations, according to what was spoken, "So shall your descendants be."*

19 *And not being weak in faith, he did not consider his own body, already dead (since he was about a hundred years old), and the deadness of Sarah's womb.*

20 *He did not waver at the promise of God through unbelief, but was strengthened in faith, giving glory to God,*

21 *and being fully convinced that what He had promised He was also able to perform.*

22 *And therefore "it was accounted to him for righteousness."*

23 *Now it was not written for his sake alone that it was imputed to him,*

24 *but also for us. It shall be imputed to us who believe in Him who raised up Jesus our Lord from the dead,*

25 *who was delivered up because of our offenses, and was raised because of our justification.*

Exploring the Meaning

5) According to this passage, what is the connection between circumcision (or any other religious ritual, for that matter) and salvation?

_____

_____

_____

_____

_____

6) Read Romans 2:28–29. What is "circumcision . . . of the heart"?

_____

_____

_____

_____

7) Read Ephesians 1:13–14. What light does this passage shed upon the timing of the indwelling of the Holy Spirit?

_____

_____

_____

_____

_____

Truth for Today

The validity of good works in God's sight depends on whose power they are done in and for whose glory. When they are done in the power of His Spirit and for His glory, they are beautiful and acceptable to Him. When they are done in the power of the flesh and for the sake of personal recognition or merit, they are rejected by Him. Legalism is separated from true obedience by attitude. The one is a rotten smell in God's nostrils, whereas the other is a sweet savor.

REFLECTING ON THE TEXT

8) Some believers fall prey to formalism, substituting external ceremonies and rites for the internal reality of personal growth in the Lord. Others fall into legalistic systems of dos and don'ts, proudly hoping to improve their standing before God by doing or not doing certain things. Still others look for a "second blessing"—a spiritual secret to unlock some higher plane of spiritual reality, hoping to receive more of God than they imagine was granted to them at conversion. To which of these errors are you most prone, and why?

_____

_____

_____

_____

_____

9) What commonly accepted rules have many Christians tried to make part of the gospel? How is this similar to what the Judaizers were doing among the Galatian believers?

_____

_____

_____

_____

_____

10) Do you know someone who—like the Galatians—is being told that faith alone won't justify them? How can you help them today break free from the bondage of trying to earn God's approval through human effort?

_____

_____

_____

_____

PERSONAL RESPONSE

Write out additional reflections, questions you may have, or a prayer.

ADDITIONAL NOTES

5

THE LAW AND THE PROMISE
Galatians 3:10–18

DRAWING NEAR

If you had to make the case for grace to a religious friend who insisted that "salvation *can't* be a free gift! Surely, we *have* to do our part!" what would you say?

— Hard to say. Our part springs out of our gift. Very hard concept to fathom/understand. But salvation is a gift. All have sinned.

What struggle with sin have you encountered this past week? How did you deal with it?

Lust and insecurity. Lust-gave in. Insecurity reflected on God's past grace.

Take some time to think about what Christ has done for you—redeemed you from sin through His death on the cross, and given you forgiveness and new life. Ask God to open your heart to what He wants to teach you.

THE CONTEXT

We've seen how Paul has refuted the Jewish legalists who infiltrated the churches. Paul saw this as nothing less than a devilish assault on the pure and simple gospel of justification by faith. After establishing his apostolic credentials, Paul made his case for justification by faith alone using a revered Old Testament person (Abraham) and assorted Old Testament passages.

Paul anticipated and refuted a possible objection to his use of Abraham to prove the doctrine of justification by faith: that the giving of the law at Sinai occurred after Abraham and brought about a change and a better method of salvation. The apostle dismissed that argument by showing the superiority of the Abrahamic covenant (vv. 15–18) and the inferiority of the law (vv. 19–22).

Paul again emphasized that there is no middle ground between law (works) and promise (grace); the two principles are mutually exclusive (see Rom. 4:14). An "inheritance" is by definition something granted, not worked for, as proven in the case of Abraham.

KEYS TO THE TEXT

Redeemed: The Greek word translated "redeemed" was often used to speak of buying a slave's or debtor's freedom. Christ's death, because it was a death of substitution for sin, satisfied God's justice and exhausted His wrath toward His elect, so that Christ actually purchased believers from slavery to sin and from the sentence of eternal death (Titus 2:14; see Rom. 3:24; Eph. 1:7). The only adequate payment to redeem sinners from sin's slavery and its deserved punishment was "in Christ Jesus" (1 Tim. 2:6; 1 Pet. 1:18, 19), and was paid to God to satisfy His justice.

Promises to Abraham: These are the promises found in the Abrahamic covenant (Gen. 12:3, 7; 13:15–16; 15:5, 18; 17:8; 22:16–18; 26:3–4; 28:13–14). Because these promises were made both to Abraham and to his descendants, they did not become void when Abraham died or when the law came. The covenant with Abraham was an unconditional covenant of promise relying solely on God's faithfulness, whereas the covenant with Moses was a conditional covenant of law relying on man's faithfulness. To Abraham, God said, "I will." Through Moses He said, "Thou shalt." The promise set forth a religion dependent on God. The law set forth a religion dependent on man. The promise centers on God's plan, God's grace, God's initiative, God's sovereignty, God's blessings. The law centers on man's duty, man's work, man's responsibility, man's behavior, man's obedience. The promise, being grounded in grace, requires only sincere faith. The law, being grounded in works, demands perfect obedience. In contrasting the covenants of promise and of law, Paul first shows the superiority of the one and then the inferiority of the other.

UNLEASHING THE TEXT

Read 3:10–18, noting the key words and definitions next to the passage.

Galatians 3:10–18 (NKJV)

10 For as many as are of the works of the law are under the curse; for it is written, "Cursed is everyone who does not continue in all things which are written in the book of the law, to do them."

11 But that no one is justified by the law in the sight of God is evident, for "the just shall live by faith."

12 Yet the law is not of faith, but "the man who does them shall live by them."

13 Christ has redeemed us from the curse of the law, having become a curse for us (for it is written, "Cursed is everyone who hangs on a tree"),

14 that the blessing of Abraham might come upon the Gentiles in Christ Jesus, that we might receive the promise of the Spirit through faith.

15 Brethren, I speak in the manner of men: Though it is only a man's covenant, yet if it is confirmed, no one annuls or adds to it.

16 Now to Abraham and his Seed were the promises made. He does not say, "And to seeds," as of many, but as of one, "And to your Seed," who is Christ.

as many as are of the works of the law (v. 10)—those attempting to earn salvation by keeping the law

under the curse (v. 10)—quoted from Deuteronomy 27:26 to show that failure to perfectly keep the law brings divine judgment and condemnation; one violation of the law deserves the curse of God (see Deut. 27–28)

all things (v. 10)—See James 2:10. No one can keep all the commands of the law—not even strict Pharisees like Saul of Tarsus.

justified (v. 11)—made righteous before God

the just shall live by faith (v. 11)—Paul's earlier Old Testament quote (v. 10; see Deut. 27:26) showed that justification does not come from keeping the law. This quote from Habakkuk 2:4 shows that justification is by faith alone.

the law is not of faith (v. 12)—Justification by faith and justification by keeping the law are mutually exclusive, as Paul's Old Testament quote from Leviticus 18:5 proves.

having become a curse for us (v. 13)—By bearing God's wrath for believers' sins on the cross, Christ took upon Himself the curse pronounced on those who violated the law.

it is written (v. 13)—the common New Testament way (used sixty-one times) of introducing Old Testament quotes

the blessing of Abraham (v. 14)—faith in God's promise of salvation

promise of the Spirit (v. 14)—from God the Father (see Isa. 32:15; Ezek. 37:14; Luke 11:13; 24:49; John 14:16, 26)

Brethren (v. 15)—This term of endearment reveals Paul's compassionate love for the Galatians, which they may have begun to question in light of his stern rebuke (vv. 1, 3).

manner of men . . . man's covenant (v. 15)—Even human covenants, once confirmed, are considered irrevocable and unchangeable; how much more a covenant made by an unchanging God (James 1:17).

Seed (v. 16)—See verse 19; the quote is from Genesis 12:7. The singular form of the Hebrew word, like its English and Greek counterparts, can be used in a collective sense, that is, to refer to a group. Paul's point is that in some Old Testament passages (for example, Gen. 3:15; 22:18), "seed" refers to the greatest of Abraham's descendants, Jesus Christ.

four hundred and thirty years (v. 17)—from Israel's sojourn in Egypt (see Exod. 12:40) to the giving of the law at Sinai (1445 BC); the law actually came 645 years after the initial promise to Abraham (2090 BC; see Gen. 12:4; 21:5; 25:26; 47:9), but the promise was repeated to Isaac (Gen. 26:24) and later to Jacob (1928 BC; Gen. 28:15); the last

17 *And this I say, that the law, which was four hundred and thirty years later, cannot annul the covenant that was confirmed before by God in Christ, that it should make the promise of no effect.*

18 *For if the inheritance is of the law, it is no longer of promise; but God gave it to Abraham by promise.*

known reaffirmation of the Abrahamic Covenant to Jacob occurred in Genesis 46:2–4 (1875 BC) just before he went to Egypt—430 years before the Mosaic Law was given.

the covenant (v. 17)—the Abrahamic covenant

confirmed before by God (v. 17)—The term means "ratified." Once God ratified the covenant officially, it had lasting authority so that nothing and no one could annul it. The Abrahamic covenant was unilateral (God made the promise to Himself), eternal (it provided for everlasting blessing), irrevocable (it will never cease), and unconditional (in that it depended on God, not man), but its complete fulfillment awaits the salvation of Israel and the millennial kingdom of Jesus Christ.

1) How does Paul contrast the law and faith? What does Paul say is the destiny of the one who fails to keep 100 percent of the law?

No one justified by the law. Cursed is those who does not do all the things in the law.

2) What does it mean that Christ "redeemed us"?

(Verses to consider: 1 Cor. 1:30; Gal. 4:3–5; Col. 1:13–14; 1 Pet. 1:18–19)

3) How did Christ become "a curse for us"?

_____

_____

_____

_____

_____

(Verses to consider: 2 Cor. 5:21; 1 Pet. 2:21–24)

GOING DEEPER

For further insight about the law and faith, read Romans 7:1–25.

Romans 7:1–25 (NKJV)

1   *Or do you not know, brethren (for I speak to those who know the law),
     that the law has dominion over a man as long as he lives?*

2   *For the woman who has a husband is bound by the law to her husband as
     long as he lives. But if the husband dies, she is released from the law of her
     husband.*

3   *So then if, while her husband lives, she marries another man, she will be
     called an adulteress; but if her husband dies, she is free from that law, so
     that she is no adulteress, though she has married another man.*

4   *Therefore, my brethren, you also have become dead to the law through
     the body of Christ, that you may be married to another—to Him who was
     raised from the dead, that we should bear fruit to God.*

5   *For when we were in the flesh, the sinful passions which were aroused by
     the law were at work in our members to bear fruit to death.*

6   *But now we have been delivered from the law, having died to what we
     were held by, so that we should serve in the newness of the Spirit and not
     in the oldness of the letter.*

7   *What shall we say then? Is the law sin? Certainly not! On the contrary, I
     would not have known sin except through the law. For I would not have
     known covetousness unless the law had said, "You shall not covet."*

8   *But sin, taking opportunity by the commandment, produced in me all
     manner of evil desire. For apart from the law sin was dead.*

9   *I was alive once without the law, but when the commandment came, sin
     revived and I died.*

10 *And the commandment, which was to bring life, I found to bring death.*

11 *For sin, taking occasion by the commandment, deceived me, and by it killed me.*

12 *Therefore the law is holy, and the commandment holy and just and good.*

13 *Has then what is good become death to me? Certainly not! But sin, that it might appear sin, was producing death in me through what is good, so that sin through the commandment might become exceedingly sinful.*

14 *For we know that the law is spiritual, but I am carnal, sold under sin.*

15 *For what I am doing, I do not understand. For what I will to do, that I do not practice; but what I hate, that I do.*

16 *If, then, I do what I will not to do, I agree with the law that it is good.*

17 *But now, it is no longer I who do it, but sin that dwells in me.*

18 *For I know that in me (that is, in my flesh) nothing good dwells; for to will is present with me, but how to perform what is good I do not find.*

19 *For the good that I will to do, I do not do; but the evil I will not to do, that I practice.*

20 *Now if I do what I will not to do, it is no longer I who do it, but sin that dwells in me.*

21 *I find then a law, that evil is present with me, the one who wills to do good.*

22 *For I delight in the law of God according to the inward man.*

23 *But I see another law in my members, warring against the law of my mind, and bringing me into captivity to the law of sin which is in my members.*

24 *O wretched man that I am! Who will deliver me from this body of death?*

25 *I thank God—through Jesus Christ our Lord! So then, with the mind I myself serve the law of God, but with the flesh the law of sin.*

Exploring the Meaning

4) In what ways do Paul's words in Romans 7 echo the principles being taught in 3:10–18?

_____

_____

_____

_____

_____

5) What struggle in the human condition does Paul speak about in verses 15–20?

_____

_____

_____

_____

_____

_____

6) Read John 7:37–39. Instead of a cold, external law, what did Jesus Christ promise those who would trust and obey Him?

_____

_____

_____

_____

_____

_____

_____

(Verses to consider: Isa. 44:3; Ezek. 36:26–27; 39:29; Joel 2:28–29)

7) Read Hebrews 10:38. How does this verse demonstrate that justification is by faith alone?

_____

_____

_____

_____

_____

_____

Truth for Today

Whether before or after Christ came to earth, salvation has always been provided only through the perfect offering of Christ on the cross. Believers who lived before the cross and never knew any specifics about Jesus were nevertheless forgiven and made right with God by faith in anticipation of Christ's sacrifice, whereas believers who live after the cross are saved by looking back to it. When Christ shed His blood, it covered sins on both sides of the cross. The old covenant goes back to the cross; the new covenant comes from it. On the one hand faith pointed forward, whereas on the other it points back.

Reflecting on the Text

8) When have you felt spiritually overwhelmed or discouraged because of your inability to live up to God's standard? How did you resolve this?

_____

_____

_____

_____

_____

9) What would Paul say to those who are frustrated by man-made "religious" standards?

_____

_____

_____

_____

10) List the names of those in your life who desperately need to know that salvation is a gift and can't be earned. Commit to pray for them. Ask God for opportunities to share Christ's message of love and grace with them.

_____

_____

_____

_____

PERSONAL RESPONSE

Write out additional reflections, questions you may have, or a prayer.

_____

_____

_____

_____

_____

_____

_____

_____

_____

_____

_____

_____

_____

_____

_____

_____

_____

_____

_____

_____

_____

_____

_____

_____

Additional Notes

6

THE PURPOSE OF THE LAW
Galatians 3:19–29

DRAWING NEAR

If people are inherently good, as many argue, why do we need policemen, jails, prisons, criminal courts, handcuffs, etc.?

Not all people keep being intentionally good. We all have been blessed with our own free will.

What laws, regulations, or ordinances do many people (even many Christians) routinely break? Why?

THE CONTEXT

Paul wrote this urgent letter to churches he had established in Asia Minor on his first missionary journey. Shortly after he had left them, these churches were targeted by Jewish legalists who, in essence, urged the believers in Christ to turn away from grace and embrace the tenets of Judaism, especially the rite of circumcision and a fanatical devotion to keeping the law of Moses. Because the eternal and theological implications of such teaching were grave, the brilliant apostle responded with clear teaching on the distinctions between law and grace.

Paul knew his readers would reason: "Well, if the law can't save us, why did God give the law in the first place? What's its purpose? And if the law has been set aside, are we free of any and all moral restraints?" The result is a clear and concise explanation of the purpose of the law. Without the law, people are incapable of seeing their depravity and need for forgiveness. When the law is obscured, grace appears less amazing than it actually is.

This section (3:19–29) ends on a wonderfully encouraging note. It speaks of the freedom that believers enjoy, the sonship they have, the unity they have been granted, and the inheritance that is theirs—not because they are able to keep God's laws but because of the grace of God that comes through faith in Christ.

KEYS TO THE TEXT

The Law: In the Bible, particularly the Old Testament, God directly established a unique law code to direct His people in their worship, in their relationship to Him, and in their social relationships with one another. Israel was not the only nation to have a law code. Such collections were common among the countries of the ancient world. The biblical law code, or the Mosaic Law, differed from other ancient Near Eastern law codes in several ways. Biblical law was different, first of all, in its origin. Throughout the ancient world, the laws of most nations were believed to originate with the gods, but they were considered intensely personal and subjective in the way they were applied. By contrast, the biblical concept asserted that law comes from God, issues from His nature, and is holy, righteous, and good. Furthermore, at the outset of God's ruling over Israel at Sinai, God the great King gave His laws. These laws were binding on His people, and He upheld them. Furthermore, His laws were universal and an expression of His love for His people (Exod. 19:5–6). If salvation has always been by faith and never by works, and if Jesus Christ fulfilled the covenant of promise to Abraham, what purpose did the Law have? Paul gives a direct and sobering answer: The purpose of the law was to demonstrate to man his total sinfulness, his inability to please God by his own works, and his need for mercy and grace. (*Nelson's New Illustrated Bible Dictionary*)

UNLEASHING THE TEXT

Read 3:19–29, noting the key words and definitions next to the passage.

was added because of transgressions (v. 19)—Paul's persuasive argument that the promise is superior to the law raises an obvious question: What was the purpose of the law? Paul's answer is that the law reveals humanity's utter sinfulness, inability to save themselves, and desperate need of a Savior—it was never intended to be the way of salvation.

Galatians 3:19–29 (NKJV)

19 *What purpose then does the law serve? It was added because of transgressions, till the Seed should come to whom the promise was made; and it was appointed through angels by the hand of a mediator.*

20 *Now a mediator does not mediate for one only, but God is one.*

through angels (v. 19)—The Bible teaches that angels were involved in the giving of the law (see Heb. 2:2) but does not explain the precise role they played.

mediator (v. 20)—Paul's point is apparently that a "mediator" is required when more than one party is involved, but God alone ratified the covenant with Abraham.

21 Is the law then against the promises of God? Certainly not! For if there had been a law given which could have given life, truly righteousness would have been by the law.

22 But the Scripture has confined all under sin, that the promise by faith in Jesus Christ might be given to those who believe.

23 But before faith came, we were kept under guard by the law, kept for the faith which would afterward be revealed.

24 Therefore the law was our tutor to bring us to Christ, that we might be justified by faith.

25 But after faith has come, we are no longer under a tutor.

26 For you are all sons of God through faith in Christ Jesus.

27 For as many of you as were baptized into Christ have put on Christ.

Certainly not! (v. 21)—Paul uses the strongest Greek negative (see 2:17) to disdain the idea that the law and the promise are at opposite purposes. Since God gave them both and does not work against Himself, law and promise work in harmony; the law reveals humans' sinfulness and need for the salvation freely offered in the promise. If the law could have provided righteousness and eternal life, there would be no gracious promise.

confined all under sin (v. 22)—The Greek verb translated "confined" means "to enclose on all sides." Paul portrays all humankind as hopelessly trapped in sin, like a school of fish caught in a net; that all people are sinners is the express teaching of Scripture (Isa. 53:6; Rom. 3:23).

before faith came (v. 23)—From the viewpoints of both the history of redemption and through all times in the area of individual salvation (vv. 19, 24–25; 4:1–4), only saving faith unlocks the door of the prison where the law keeps men and women bound.

kept under guard by the law (v. 23)—Paul personifies the law as a jailer of guilty, condemned sinners, on death row awaiting God's judgment.

the faith which would afterward be revealed (v. 23)—Again, Paul was looking at the coming of Christ historically, and at each believer's salvation individually. Faith in Christ alone releases people from bondage to law, whether the Mosaic Law or the law written on the hearts of Gentiles.

tutor (v. 24)—The Greek word denotes a slave who had the duty of taking care of a child until adulthood. The "tutor" would escort the children to and from school and watch over their behavior at home. Tutors were often strict disciplinarians, causing those under their care to yearn for the day when they would be free from their tutor's custody. The law, our tutor, was escorting us to Christ by showing us our sins.

sons of God (v. 26)—While God is the Father of all people in a general sense because He created them (Acts 17:24–28), only those who have put their faith in Jesus Christ are God's true spiritual children; unbelievers are the children of Satan (1 John 3:10).

baptized into Christ (v. 27)—This is not water baptism, which cannot save. Paul used the word "baptized" in a metaphorical manner to speak of being "placed into" Christ (see 2:20) by the spiritual miracle of union with Him in His death and resurrection.

put on Christ (v. 27)—the result of the believer's spiritual union with Christ; Paul was emphasizing the fact that we have been united with Christ through salvation; positionally before God, we have put on Christ, His death, resurrection, and righteousness; practically, we need to "put on Christ" before people in our conduct (Rom. 13:14).

you are all one in Christ Jesus (v. 28)—All those who are one with Jesus Christ are one with each other. This verse does not deny that God has designed racial, social, and sexual distinctions among Christians, but it affirms that those distinctions do not imply spiritual inequality before God; nor is this spiritual equality incompatible with the God-ordained roles of headship and submission in the church, society, and at home. Jesus Christ, though fully equal with the Father, assumed a submissive role during His incarnation (Phil. 2:5–8).

28 There is neither Jew nor Greek, there is neither slave nor free, there is neither male nor female; for you are all one in Christ Jesus.

29 And if you are Christ's, then you are Abraham's seed, and heirs according to the promise.

1) Underline every word or phrase that refers to or describes the law. How does Paul describe the law in this passage? What does he suggest is its purpose?

_____

_____

_____

_____

2) What does this passage say about the universality of sin or the depravity of the human race? Is anyone able to keep the perfect law of God? Why or why not?

_____

_____

_____

(Verses to consider: 1 Kin. 8:46; Ps. 143:2; Rom. 3:9–23)

3) Reread verses 25–29 and list everything that Paul says *every* believer is and has—no matter what their gender, race, or station in life.

_____

_____

_____

(Verses to consider: Rom. 8:14–17)

4) What does it mean to be "baptized into Christ" (v. 27)?

_____

_____

_____

(Verses to consider: Rom. 6:3–5)

GOING DEEPER

Jesus also spoke about the law. Read what he said in Matthew 5:17–48.

Matthew 5:17–48 (NKJV)

17 *Do not think that I came to destroy the Law or the Prophets. I did not come to destroy but to fulfill.*

18 *For assuredly, I say to you, till heaven and earth pass away, one jot or one tittle will by no means pass from the law till all is fulfilled.*

19 *Whoever therefore breaks one of the least of these commandments, and teaches men so, shall be called least in the kingdom of heaven; but whoever does and teaches them, he shall be called great in the kingdom of heaven.*

20 *For I say to you, that unless your righteousness exceeds the righteousness of the scribes and Pharisees, you will by no means enter the kingdom of heaven.*

21 *You have heard that it was said to those of old, "You shall not murder, and whoever murders will be in danger of the judgment."*

22 *But I say to you that whoever is angry with his brother without a cause shall be in danger of the judgment. And whoever says to his brother, "Raca!" shall be in danger of the council. But whoever says, "You fool!" shall be in danger of hell fire.*

23 *Therefore if you bring your gift to the altar, and there remember that your brother has something against you,*

24 *leave your gift there before the altar, and go your way. First be reconciled to your brother, and then come and offer your gift.*

25 *Agree with your adversary quickly, while you are on the way with him, lest your adversary deliver you to the judge, the judge hand you over to the officer, and you be thrown into prison.*

26 *Assuredly, I say to you, you will by no means get out of there till you have paid the last penny.*

27 *You have heard that it was said to those of old, "You shall not commit adultery."*

28 *But I say to you that whoever looks at a woman to lust for her has already committed adultery with her in his heart.*

29 *If your right eye causes you to sin, pluck it out and cast it from you; for it is more profitable for you that one of your members perish, than for your whole body to be cast into hell.*

30 *And if your right hand causes you to sin, cut it off and cast it from you; for it is more profitable for you that one of your members perish, than for your whole body to be cast into hell.*

31 *Furthermore it has been said, "Whoever divorces his wife, let him give her a certificate of divorce."*

32 *But I say to you that whoever divorces his wife for any reason except sexual immorality causes her to commit adultery; and whoever marries a woman who is divorced commits adultery.*

33 *Again you have heard that it was said to those of old, "You shall not swear falsely, but shall perform your oaths to the Lord."*

34 *But I say to you, do not swear at all: neither by heaven, for it is God's throne;*

35 *nor by the earth, for it is His footstool; nor by Jerusalem, for it is the city of the great King.*

36 *Nor shall you swear by your head, because you cannot make one hair white or black.*

37 *But let your "Yes" be "Yes," and your "No," "No." For whatever is more than these is from the evil one.*

38 *You have heard that it was said, "An eye for an eye and a tooth for a tooth."*

39 *But I tell you not to resist an evil person. But whoever slaps you on your right cheek, turn the other to him also.*

40 *If anyone wants to sue you and take away your tunic, let him have your cloak also.*

41 *And whoever compels you to go one mile, go with him two.*

42 *Give to him who asks you, and from him who wants to borrow from you do not turn away.*

43 *You have heard that it was said, "You shall love your neighbor and hate your enemy."*

44 *But I say to you, love your enemies, bless those who curse you, do good to those who hate you, and pray for those who spitefully use you and persecute you,*

45 *that you may be sons of your Father in heaven; for He makes His sun rise on the evil and on the good, and sends rain on the just and on the unjust.*

46 *For if you love those who love you, what reward have you? Do not even the tax collectors do the same?*

47 *And if you greet your brethren only, what do you do more than others? Do not even the tax collectors do so?*

48 *Therefore you shall be perfect, just as your Father in heaven is perfect.*

EXPLORING THE MEANING

5) What main point does Jesus make as he contrasts what the "law says" with what "He says"?

_____

_____

_____

_____

6) How do you think the Jewish religious leaders felt when they heard Jesus require not only perfect *external* but also absolute *internal* conformity to the law of God?

_____

_____

_____

_____

7) Read Romans 6:23. How does the image there fit with the description in Galatians 3 of being "kept under guard by the law," of the law serving as a kind of death-row prison?

_____

_____

_____

8) Read Romans 2:12–16. How does the law written on the hearts of Gentiles compare with the law revealed by God through Moses?

_____

_____

_____

Truth for Today

The covenant of law is long past, but the moral demands of the law have not diminished, having neither begun nor ended with the Mosaic covenant. That is why preaching the moral, ethical standards of the law today is still imperative in driving men to Christ. Unless men realize they are living in violation of God's law and therefore stand under His divine judgment, they will see no reason to be saved. Grace is meaningless to a person who feels no inadequacy or need of help. He sees no purpose in being saved if he does not realize he is lost. He sees no need of forgiveness by God if he does not know he has offended God. He sees no need to seek God's mercy if he is unaware he is under God's wrath. The purpose of the law was, and is, to drive men to despair over their sins and to a desire to receive the salvation that God's sovereign grace offers to those who believe.

Reflecting on the Text

9) John Stott has written: "We cannot come to Christ to be justified until we have first been to Moses to be condemned. But once we have gone to Moses, and acknowledged our sin, guilt, and condemnation, we must not stay there. We must let Moses send us to Christ." Instead of the futility of trying to keep the impossible demands of the law, Paul urges believers to "put on Christ" (Gal. 3:27; also see Rom. 13:14). How does one do this? What would "putting on Christ" look like in your life today?

_____

_____

_____

_____

_____

10) What are some of the blessings of being a "son/daughter of God"? How can you live in such a way today that your Father is honored and glorified?

_____

_____

_____

_____

_____

11) What central truth stands out in your mind from this lesson?
Summarize that idea in your own words.

_____

_____

_____

_____

_____

Personal Response

Write out additional reflections, questions you may have, or a prayer.

_____

_____

_____

_____

_____

_____

_____

_____

_____

_____

_____

_____

_____

_____

_____

_____

_____

ADDITIONAL NOTES

_____

_____

_____

_____

_____

_____

_____

_____

_____

_____

_____

_____

_____

_____

_____

_____

_____

_____

_____

_____

_____

_____

_____

_____

_____

_____

_____

_____

7

CHILDREN OF GOD
Galatians 4:1–11

DRAWING NEAR

A conversation with a neighbor turns to spiritual things. At one point your neighbor exclaims, "Well, I believe we're all children of God. He created us all and loves us all, whether we're Christian, Jewish, Hindu, or Muslim." How would you respond?

_____

_____

_____

What does it mean that God has adopted you? How does God's Spirit confirm this fact in your life?

_____

_____

_____

THE CONTEXT

Continuing his basic argument that salvation is not gained by human merit but solely by God's sovereign grace through faith, Paul further developed the analogy of a child becoming an adult (3:23–26). He compared the position and privileges of a child to those of a servant, with the figures of child and servant representing life under the law and the figures of adult and son representing life in Christ. Both Paul's Jewish and Gentile readers readily understood this imagery, since the Jews, Greeks, and Romans all had a ceremony to celebrate a person's coming of age.

While salvation is the free gift of God, it brings with it serious responsibility. God requires believers to live holy lives because they are children of a holy God. This obligation to the unchanging moral and spiritual principles that forever reflect the nature of God, however, does not include the rituals and ceremonies unique to Israel under Mosaic Law, as the Judaizers falsely claimed. The central truths of 4:1–11 are that life under law is meant by God to be preparation for divine sonship, and that trust in His grace brings realization of that sonship.

KEYS TO THE TEXT

Adoption: Using the figure of adoption, Paul explains the believer's intimate and permanent relationship to God as a beloved child. The term *adoption* abounds with the ideas of love, grace, compassion, and intimate relationship. It is the action by which a husband and wife decide to take a boy or girl who is not their physical offspring into their family as their own child. When accomplished by the proper legal means, the adoption grants the child all the rights and privileges of a member of the family. Since unregenerate people are by nature children of the devil, the only way they can become God's children is by spiritual adoption. God confirms the believer's eternal relation to Him as His child, testifying that we are each led, given access to God, and granted inner assurance by His own Holy Spirit.

God's Heirs: God has provided an incomprehensible wealth of riches for those who love His Son. The treasures He has prepared are infinite. Jesus said, "The kingdom of heaven is like treasure hidden in a field, which a man found and hid; and for joy over it goes and sells all that he has, and buys that field" (Matt. 13:44). The apostle Paul quotes the prophet Isaiah when he says, "Eye has not seen, nor ear heard, nor have entered into the heart of man the things which God has prepared for those who love him" (1 Cor. 2:9). The good news is, if we love the Son of God, we inherit all the riches of the Father. If we believe in Christ, we have treasure beyond imagination.

UNLEASHING THE TEXT

Read 4:1–11, noting the key words and definitions next to the passage.

child (v. 1)—The Greek word refers to a child too young to talk; a minor, spiritually and intellectually immature and not ready for the privileges and responsibilities of adulthood.

guardians and stewards (v. 2)—"Guardians" were slaves entrusted with the care of under-age boys, while "stewards" managed property for the boys until they came of age. Along with the tutor (3:24), they had almost complete charge of the child—so that, for all practical purposes, a child under their care did not differ from a slave.

Galatians 4:1–11 (NKJV)

1 *Now I say that the heir, as long as he is a child, does not differ at all from a slave, though he is master of all,*

2 *but is under guardians and stewards until the time appointed by the father.*

3 *Even so we, when we were children, were in bondage under the elements of the world.*

4 *But when the fullness of the time had come, God sent forth His Son, born of a woman, born under the law,*

5 *to redeem those who were under the law, that we might receive the adoption as sons.*

6 *And because you are sons, God has sent forth the Spirit of His Son into your hearts, crying out, "Abba, Father!"*

7 *Therefore you are no longer a slave but a son, and if a son, then an heir of God through Christ.*

8 *But then, indeed, when you did not know God, you served those which by nature are not gods.*

when we were children . . . in bondage (v. 3)—before our "coming of age" when we came to saving faith in Jesus Christ

the elements of the world (v. 3)—"Elements" is from a Greek word meaning "row," or "rank," and was used to speak of basic, foundational things like the letters of the alphabet. In light of its use in verse 9, it is best to see it here as a reference to the basic elements and rituals of human religion. Paul describes both Jewish and Gentile religions as elemental because they are merely human, never rising to the level of the divine. Both Jewish religion and Gentile religion centered on human-made systems of works; they were filled with laws and ceremonies to be performed so as to achieve divine acceptance. All such rudimentary elements are immature, like behaviors of children under bondage to a guardian.

the fullness of the time (v. 4)—In God's timetable, when the exact religious, cultural, and political conditions demanded by His perfect plan were in place, Jesus came into the world.

God sent forth His Son (v. 4)—Just as a father would set the time for the ceremony of his son coming of age and being released from the guardians, stewards, and tutors, so God sent His Son at the precise moment to bring all who believe out from under bondage to the law—a truth Jesus repeatedly affirmed (John 5:30, 36–37; 8:16, 18, 42; 12:49; 17:21, 25; 20:21). That the Father sent Jesus into the world implies Jesus's preexistence as the eternal second member of the Trinity.

born of a woman (v. 4)—This emphasizes Jesus's full humanity, not merely His virgin birth (Isa. 7:14; Matt. 1:20–25). Jesus had to be fully God for His sacrifice to be of the infinite worth needed to atone for sin, but He also had to be fully man so He could take upon Himself the penalty of sin as the substitute for human beings.

under the law (v. 4)—Like all human beings, Jesus was obligated to obey God's law. Unlike anyone else, however, He perfectly obeyed that law (1 John 3:5). His sinlessness made Him the unblemished sacrifice for sins, who "fulfilled all righteousness" (that is, perfectly obeyed God in everything). That perfect righteousness is what is imputed to those who believe in Him.

those . . . under the law (v. 5)—guilty sinners who are under the law's demands and its curses and in need of a savior

Spirit of His Son (v. 6)—It is the Holy Spirit's work to confirm to believers their adoption as God's children. Assurance of salvation is a gracious work of the Holy Spirit and does not come from any human source.

Abba (v. 6)—an Aramaic term of endearment, used by young children to speak to their fathers; the equivalent of the word "Daddy"

when you did not know God (v. 8)—Before coming to saving faith in Christ, no unsaved person knows God.

by nature are not gods (v. 8)—the Greco-Roman pantheon of nonexistent deities the Galatians had imagined they worshiped before their conversion (see Rom. 1:23; 1 Cor. 8:4; 10:19–20; 12:2; 1 Thess. 1:9)

known by God (v. 9)—We can know God only because He first knew us, just as we choose Him only because He first chose us (John 6:44; 15:16), and we love Him only because He first loved us (1 John 4:19).

days . . . years (v. 10)—the rituals, ceremonies, and festivals of the Jewish religious calendar that God had given to Israel but were never required for the church; Paul warns the Galatians, as he did the Colossians, against legalistically observing them as if they were required by God or could earn favor with Him.

labored . . . in vain (v. 11)—Paul feared that his effort in establishing and building the Galatian churches might prove to be futile if they fell back into legalism.

9 *But now after you have known God, or rather are known by God, how is it that you turn again to the weak and beggarly elements, to which you desire again to be in bondage?*

10 *You observe days and months and seasons and years.*

11 *I am afraid for you, lest I have labored for you in vain.*

1) How has being under the law prepared us for sonship? To what ancient practice is Paul referring when he implies that the law functioned as a guardian or manager?

_____

_____

_____

_____

_____

_____

2) Like all humanity, Jesus was born under the law (v. 4). But how was Christ different from other people in his relationship and response to the law?

_____

_____

_____

_____

_____

_____

(Verses to consider: John 8:46; 2 Cor. 5:21; Heb. 4:15; 7:26; 1 Pet. 2:22)

3) What does it mean to you to call God your Father, or your Daddy?

_____

_____

_____

_____

_____

_____

_____

4) What concern did Paul express over the Galatians and their legalistic behavior?

_____

_____

_____

_____

_____

_____

_____

GOING DEEPER

Again, Paul's teaching in the book of Romans sheds light on this topic in Galatians. Read Romans 8:1–17.

Romans 8:1–17 (NKJV)

1 *There is therefore now no condemnation to those who are in Christ Jesus, who do not walk according to the flesh, but according to the Spirit.*

2 *For the law of the Spirit of life in Christ Jesus has made me free from the law of sin and death.*

3 *For what the law could not do in that it was weak through the flesh, God did by sending His own Son in the likeness of sinful flesh, on account of sin: He condemned sin in the flesh,*

4   *that the righteous requirement of the law might be fulfilled in us who do not walk according to the flesh but according to the Spirit.*

5   *For those who live according to the flesh set their minds on the things of the flesh, but those who live according to the Spirit, the things of the Spirit.*

6   *For to be carnally minded is death, but to be spiritually minded is life and peace.*

7   *Because the carnal mind is enmity against God; for it is not subject to the law of God, nor indeed can be.*

8   *So then, those who are in the flesh cannot please God.*

9   *But you are not in the flesh but in the Spirit, if indeed the Spirit of God dwells in you. Now if anyone does not have the Spirit of Christ, he is not His.*

10   *And if Christ is in you, the body is dead because of sin, but the Spirit is life because of righteousness.*

11   *But if the Spirit of Him who raised Jesus from the dead dwells in you, He who raised Christ from the dead will also give life to your mortal bodies through His Spirit who dwells in you.*

12   *Therefore, brethren, we are debtors—not to the flesh, to live according to the flesh.*

13   *For if you live according to the flesh you will die; but if by the Spirit you put to death the deeds of the body, you will live.*

14   *For as many as are led by the Spirit of God, these are sons of God.*

15   *For you did not receive the spirit of bondage again to fear, but you received the Spirit of adoption by whom we cry out, "Abba, Father."*

16   *The Spirit Himself bears witness with our spirit that we are children of God,*

17   *and if children, then heirs—heirs of God and joint heirs with Christ, if indeed we suffer with Him, that we may also be glorified together.*

EXPLORING THE MEANING

5) What additional insights into sonship does Romans 8 add to the teaching of Galatians 3?

_____

_____

_____

_____

_____

6) Note how many times the "Spirit" is mentioned and all that the Holy Spirit does. What does this tell you about how you can grow spiritually?

_____

_____

_____

_____

_____

_____

7) Read Ephesians 4:17–19. Is it possible to know God apart from believing in Christ? Why or why not?

_____

_____

_____

_____

_____

_____

(Verses to consider: John 8:28–47; 2 Cor. 4:3–6; Eph 2:1–10; 1 John 4:19)

8) Read Romans 14:1–8, 14–18. Are any Jewish rituals, customs, or holy days required for the church and modern-day believers? How do you know?

_____

_____

_____

_____

_____

_____

(Verses to consider: Col. 2:16–17)

TRUTH FOR TODAY

Because believers are God's children, they are then "heirs of God and joint heirs with Christ" (Rom. 8:17). What an incomprehensible truth: that by giving ourselves to Jesus Christ in faith, God gives us everything His Son possesses! The gracious gift of sonship is free, but it brings serious obligation. Great blessing carries great responsibility (Luke 12:48).

REFLECTING ON THE TEXT

9) How do you know that you are a child of God? How can you be sure? How can any believer have assurance?

_____

_____

_____

_____

_____

10) How faithfully are you living as an adopted heir of the King of the universe? What practical difference should this biblical truth make in your life today?

_____

_____

_____

_____

_____

11) What "weak and worthless elemental things" are you tempted to follow in order to please God or somehow "earn" His approval? Ask God for discernment in knowing how to honor Him.

_____

_____

_____

_____

Personal Response

Write out additional reflections, questions you may have, or a prayer.

ADDITIONAL NOTES

8

CHRIST IN YOU
Galatians 4:12–20

DRAWING NEAR

In speaking against falsehood and telling the truth to the Galatian Christians, Paul took a risk. Have you ever told someone you love a hard truth about something in their lives? What happened?

Not Really

How has your understanding of living by grace grown during this study of Galatians?

Maybe

THE CONTEXT

Until this point, Paul's approach has been confrontational and impersonal. He has been writing like a scholar or debater, marshaling every possible argument and illustration to get his message across. He has taken the stance of a determined lawyer in court or a learned theologian in the classroom, giving a dispassionate and irrefutable presentation. He has referred to the Old Testament to teach the Galatians the basic truth of the gospel that he had taught them many times before: Salvation is by God's grace through faith alone. He has used both his own experience and that of the Galatians to reinforce his teaching. But for the most part, he has sounded detached, seeming to be more concerned about principles than people.

The apostle's approach changed dramatically in 4:12, moving from the purely doctrinal to the more personal. In fact, verses 12–20 are Paul's strongest words of personal affection in any of his letters. He did not so much preach or teach as simply pour out his heart in personal exhortation. He wrote, in effect, "I care about you more than I can say. I love you dearly just as you have loved me dearly. Please listen to what I'm saying, because it's so vitally essential." Take a closer look at this passage.

Keys to the Text

Formed in Christ's Image: The Greek verb for "formed" (*morphoō*) carries the idea of essential form rather than outward shape, and therefore refers to Christlike character. Christlikeness is the goal of the believer's life. "As you therefore have received Christ Jesus the Lord, so walk in Him," Paul said (Col. 2:6). God has predestined believers "to become conformed to the image of His Son" (Rom. 8:29). "We all, with unveiled face beholding as in a mirror the glory of the Lord, are being transformed into the same image from glory to glory, just as from the Lord, the Spirit" (2 Cor. 3:18). The Father sent the Son to earth not only to die that men might be saved but also to live as the divine example for those who are saved. Paul sought to bring the Galatians to Christlikeness—the goal of salvation.

Unleashing the Text

Read 4:12–20, noting the key words and definitions next to the passage.

become like me, for I became like you (v. 12)—Paul had been a proud, self-righteous Pharisee, trusting in his own righteousness to save him (see Phil. 3:4–6). But when he came to Christ, he abandoned all efforts to save himself, trusting wholly in God's grace (Phil. 3:7–9). He urged the Galatians to follow his example and avoid the legalism of the Judaizers.

You have not injured me (v. 12)—Though the Jews had persecuted him during his first trip to Galatia, the Galatian believ-

Galatians 4:12–20 (NKJV)

12 Brethren, I urge you to become like me, for I became like you. You have not injured me at all.

13 You know that because of physical infirmity I preached the gospel to you at the first.

14 And my trial which was in my flesh you did not despise or reject, but you received me as an angel of God, even as Christ Jesus.

15 What then was the blessing you enjoyed? For I bear you witness that, if possible, you would have plucked out your own eyes and given them to me.

ers had not harmed Paul. Instead, they had enthusiastically received him when he preached the gospel to them (see Acts 14:19), so he asked how they could reject him now.

physical infirmity (v. 13)—Some think the illness to which Paul was referring was malaria, possibly contracted in the coastal lowlands of Pamphylia. That could explain why Paul and Barnabas apparently did not preach at Perga, a city in Pamphylia (see Acts 13:13–14). The cooler and healthier weather in Galatia and especially at Pisidian Antioch (3,600 feet above sea level), where Paul went when he left Perga, would have brought some relief to the fever caused by malaria. Although malaria is a serious, debilitating disease, its attacks are not continuous; Paul could have ministered between bouts.

you received me (v. 14)—The Galatians had welcomed Paul in spite of his illness, which in no way had been a barrier to his credibility or acceptance.

blessing you enjoyed (v. 15)—"Blessing" can also be translated "happiness" or "satisfaction." Paul points out that the Galatians had been happy and content with his gospel preaching (see Acts 13:48), so he wondered why they had turned against him.

16 Have I therefore become your _enemy_ because _I tell you the truth?_

17 They zealously court you, but for no good; yes, they want to exclude you, _that you may be zealous for them._

18 But it is good to be _zealous_ in a _good thing always_, and not only when I am present with you.

19 My little children, for whom I labor in birth again until Christ is formed in you,

20 _I would like to be present with you now and to change my tone; for I have doubts about you._

plucked out your own eyes (v. 15)—This may be a figure of speech (see Matt. 18:9) or an indication that Paul's bodily illness had somehow affected his eyes (see Gal. 6:11). In either case, it reflects the great love the Galatians had initially expressed for the apostle.

your enemy (v. 16)—The Galatians had become so confused that, despite their previous affection for Paul, some had come to regard him as their enemy. The apostle reminds them that he had not harmed them but merely had told them the truth—a truth that had once brought them great joy.

They (v. 17)—the Judaizers

zealously (v. 17)—with a serious concern, or warm interest (the same word is used in 1:14 to describe Paul's former zeal for Judaism); the Judaizers appeared to have a genuine interest in the Galatians, but their true motive was to exclude the Galatians from God's gracious salvation and win recognition for themselves.

not only when I am present (v. 18)—Paul encouraged the Galatians to have the same zeal for the true gospel of grace that they had had when he was with them.

My little children (v. 19)—Paul's only use of this affectionate phrase, which John uses frequently (1 John 2:1, 18, 28; 3:7; 4:4; 5:21)

doubts (v. 20)—The verb means "to be at wits end" (see v. 6).

1) When Paul urged the Galatians to "become as I am," did he mean they were to: (a) become missionaries; (b) become free from the pressure to conform to the law; (c) become circumcised? How do you know?

B. We are free from the pressures of the law through

(Verses to consider: 1 Cor. 9:20–22; Gal. 2:19; 5:1; Eph. 2:6–10)

75

2) What memories of his time in Galatia did Paul relate? What is significant about these actions on the part of the Galatian church?

How welcoming the church was and now some treat him like an enemy

(Verses to consider: Acts 13:43–14:1)

3) How does Paul's analogy in verse 19 shed light on his feelings for the Galatians?

He loves them / pheubty.

GOING DEEPER

The Pharisees and scribes were known for their legalism and rigid adherence to the law, like the Judaizers Paul talks about in Galatians. Read Matthew 23:1–28 to see what Jesus said about their hearts.

Matthew 23:1–28 (NKJV)

1 *Then Jesus spoke to the multitudes and to His disciples,*
2 *saying: "The scribes and the Pharisees sit in Moses' seat.*
3 *"Therefore whatever they tell you to observe, that observe and do, but do not do according to their works; for they say, and do not do.*
4 *For they bind heavy burdens, hard to bear, and lay them on men's shoulders; but they themselves will not move them with one of their fingers.*

5   *"But all their works they do to be seen by men. They make their phylacteries broad and enlarge the borders of their garments.*

6   *They love the best places at feasts, the best seats in the synagogues,*

7   *greetings in the marketplaces, and to be called by men, 'Rabbi, Rabbi.'*

8   *"But you, do not be called 'Rabbi'; for One is your Teacher, the Christ, and you are all brethren.*

9   *Do not call anyone on earth your father; for One is your Father, He who is in heaven.*

10 *"And do not be called teachers; for One is your Teacher, the Christ.*

11 *But he who is greatest among you shall be your servant.*

12 *And whoever exalts himself will be humbled, and he who humbles himself will be exalted.*

13 *"But woe to you, scribes and Pharisees, hypocrites! For you shut up the kingdom of heaven against men; for you neither go in yourselves, nor do you allow those who are entering to go in.*

14 *Woe to you, scribes and Pharisees, hypocrites! For you devour widows' houses, and for a pretense make long prayers. Therefore you will receive greater condemnation.*

15 *"Woe to you, scribes and Pharisees, hypocrites! For you travel land and sea to win one proselyte, and when he is won, you make him twice as much a son of hell as yourselves.*

16 *"Woe to you, blind guides, who say, 'Whoever swears by the temple, it is nothing; but whoever swears by the gold of the temple, he is obliged to perform it.'*

17 *Fools and blind! For which is greater, the gold or the temple that sanctifies the gold?*

18 *And, 'Whoever swears by the altar, it is nothing; but whoever swears by the gift that is on it, he is obliged to perform it.'*

19 *Fools and blind! For which is greater, the gift or the altar that sanctifies the gift?*

20 *Therefore he who swears by the altar, swears by it and by all things on it.*

21 *He who swears by the temple, swears by it and by Him who dwells in it.*

22 *And he who swears by heaven, swears by the throne of God and by Him who sits on it.*

23 *"Woe to you, scribes and Pharisees, hypocrites! For you pay tithe of mint and anise and cummin, and have neglected the weightier matters of the law: justice and mercy and faith. These you ought to have done, without leaving the others undone.*

24 *Blind guides, who strain out a gnat and swallow a camel!*

25 "Woe to you, scribes and Pharisees, hypocrites! For you cleanse the outside of the cup and dish, but inside they are full of extortion and self-indulgence.

26 Blind Pharisee, first cleanse the inside of the cup and dish, that the outside of them may be clean also.

27 "Woe to you, scribes and Pharisees, hypocrites! For you are like whitewashed tombs which indeed appear beautiful outwardly, but inside are full of dead men's bones and all uncleanness.

28 Even so you also outwardly appear righteous to men, but inside you are full of hypocrisy and lawlessness."

EXPLORING THE MEANING

4) How are the scribes and Pharisees of Matthew 23 similar to the Judaizers as described by Paul in Galatians?

_____

_____

_____

_____

_____

_____

5) Why did Paul (and Jesus) risk making enemies or hurting people's feelings to speak the truth?

_____

_____

_____

_____

_____

_____

_____

6) Read 1 Thessalonians 2:7–8. How do Paul's tender words here echo Paul's heart as revealed in Galatians 4:19–20? How do these passages square with the common misperception of Paul as being an insensitive and impatient minister of the gospel?

_____

_____

_____

_____

_____

_____

7) Read Romans 8:29. In light of this verse and Galatians 4:19, what is God's goal for believers? What does that mean?

_____

_____

_____

_____

_____

_____

_____

(Verses to consider: Rom. 13:14; 2 Cor. 3:18; Col. 1:28; 2:6; 1 John 3:2)

TRUTH FOR TODAY

The seeds of Christlikeness are planted at the moment of conversion. Colossians 2:10 says we are made "complete" in Christ. Peter adds that believers have been granted "all things that pertain unto life and godliness" (2 Pet. 1:3). If you are a

Christian, the life of God dwells in your soul, and with it all that you need for heaven. The principle of eternal life is already in you, meaning you have claim to heaven as a present possession. You have already passed from death to life (John 5:24). You are a new person. Whereas you were once enslaved to sin, you have now become a slave of righteousness (Rom. 6:18). Instead of receiving the wages of sin, which is death, you have received God's gift of eternal life (Rom. 6:23). And eternal life means abundant life (John 10:10). It is like an artesian well of spiritual power within us, satisfying and enabling us to live the life to which God calls us (John 7:38). As Paul writes, "If any man be in Christ, he is a new creature: old things are passed away; behold, all things are become new" (2 Cor. 5:17).

REFLECTING ON THE TEXT

8) Has someone ever told you the truth about yourself or about a situation you were in, even though it was hard to hear? How did you respond?

_____

_____

_____

_____

_____

9) In what ways are you becoming more Christlike? What are some tangible evidences of the supernatural, transforming work of the Spirit of God in your life? What are some glaring areas in which you still need to change?

_____

_____

_____

_____

_____

_____

PERSONAL RESPONSE

Write out additional reflections, questions you may have, or a prayer.

Additional Notes

9

CHILDREN OF PROMISE
Galatians 4:21–5:1

DRAWING NEAR

As God's children, we are heirs of many great promises. What particular promises of God have been meaningful to you recently? Why?

Grace. No matter what happens or what we do. Christ has covered our sins

Paul reminded the Galatians about their freedom in Jesus. What does it mean to you that Christ has made you "free"?

We no longer have to be consumed by the law.

THE CONTEXT

In this next portion of Galatians, Paul—continuing to contrast grace and law, faith and works—employed an Old Testament story as an analogy or illustration of what he had been teaching. Specifically he compared the two sons of Abraham, Ishmael, and Isaac.

Many years after God first promised a son to Abraham, Sarah had not yet conceived. Abraham was old and he feared that, according to the custom of the day, his chief servant, Eliezer of Damascus, would be his only heir. He cried out to God in despair, and the Lord reaffirmed His original promise, saying, "This one shall not be your heir; but one who will come from your own body, shall be your heir" (Gen. 15:1–4). But when, after several more years, Sarah still was barren, she induced Abraham to father a child by her female slave, Hagar.

The birth of Hagar's son, Ishmael, was "according to the flesh," not because it was physical but because the scheme was motivated by purely selfish desires and fulfilled by purely human means. The birth of Isaac, however, was "through the promise." His conception was supernatural, in the sense that God miraculously enabled Abraham and Sarah to produce a child after she was far past normal childbearing age and had been barren all her life. When Isaac was born, his father was 100 and his mother was 90 (Gen. 17:17; 21:5).

The conception of Ishmael represents humanity's way, the way of the flesh, whereas that of Isaac represents God's way, the way of promise. The first is analogous to the way of religious self-effort and works righteousness. The one is the way of legalism; the other is the way of grace. Ishmael symbolizes those who have had only natural birth and who trust in their own works. Isaac symbolizes those who also had spiritual birth because they have trusted in the work of Jesus Christ.

KEYS TO THE TEXT

Old and New Covenants: The word "covenant" is from the Greek word *diathēkē*, a general term for a binding agreement, sometimes translated "testament." A covenant always involves two or more specific parties, although the terms may be stipulated and fulfilled by only one. The Old Testament consistently uses the term to refer to God's covenants with His people—covenants that God alone initiated and established and that sometimes were conditional and sometimes not. Through Moses, God gave the "old covenant" of law at Mount Sinai and required His chosen people, the Jews, to keep all the commands He gave in conjunction with that covenant. The "new covenant" was made through Jesus's death and resurrection and is a covenant of salvation by faith and grace. Paul uses the two mothers, their two sons, and the two locations as a further illustration of two covenants. Hagar, Ishmael, and Mount Sinai (earthly Jerusalem) represent the covenant of law; Sarah, Isaac, and the heavenly Jerusalem represent the covenant of promise.

UNLEASHING THE TEXT

Read 4:21–5:1, noting the key words and definitions next to the passage.

two sons (v. 22)—Ishmael, son of Sarah's Egyptian maid Hagar (Gen. 16:1–16), and Isaac, Sarah's son (Gen. 21:1–7)

according to the flesh (v. 23)—Ishmael's birth was motivated by Abraham and Sarah's lack of faith in God's promise and fulfilled by sinful human means.

through promise (v. 23)—God miraculously enabled Abraham and Sarah to have Isaac when Sarah was well past childbearing age and had been barren her entire life.

Galatians 4:21–5:1 (NKJV)

21 *Tell me, you who desire to be under the law, do you not hear the law?*

22 *For it is written that Abraham had two sons: the one by a bondwoman, the other by a freewoman.*

23 *But he who was of the bondwoman was born according to the flesh, and he of the freewoman through promise,*

24 *which things are symbolic. For these are the two covenants: the one from Mount Sinai which gives birth to bondage, which is Hagar—*

25 *for this Hagar is Mount Sinai in Arabia, and corresponds to Jerusalem which now is, and is in bondage with her children—*

26 *but the Jerusalem above is free, which is the mother of us all.*

27 *For it is written: "Rejoice, O barren, You who do not bear! Break forth and shout, You who are not in labor! For the desolate has many more children Than she who has a husband."*

28 *Now we, brethren, as Isaac was, are children of promise.*

29 *But, as he who was born according to the flesh then persecuted him who was born according to the Spirit, even so it is now.*

30 *Nevertheless what does the Scripture say? "Cast out the bondwoman and her son, for the son of the bondwoman shall not be heir with the son of the freewoman."*

31 *So then, brethren, we are not children of the bondwoman but of the free.*

symbolic (v. 24)—The Greek word was used of a story that conveyed a meaning beyond the literal sense of the words. In this passage, Paul uses historical people and places from the Old Testament to illustrate spiritual truth. This is not an allegory, nor are there any allegories in Scripture—an allegory is a fictional story where real truth is the secret, mysterious, hidden meaning. The story of Abraham, Sarah, Hagar, Ishmael, and Isaac is actual history and has no secret or hidden meaning. Paul uses it only as an illustration to support his contrast between law and grace.

Mount Sinai (v. 24)—an appropriate symbol for the old covenant, since it was at Mount Sinai that Moses received the law (Exod. 19)

Hagar (v. 24)—Since she was Sarah's slave (Gen. 16:1), Hagar is a fitting illustration of those under bondage to the law (see Gal. 3:5, 21, 23). She was actually associated with Mount Sinai through her son Ishmael, whose descendants settled in that region.

corresponds to Jerusalem (v. 25)—The law was given at Sinai and received its highest expression in the temple worship at Jerusalem. The Jewish people were still in bondage to the law.

Jerusalem above is free (v. 26)—heaven (Heb. 12:18, 22); those who are citizens of heaven (Phil. 3:20) are free from the Mosaic Law, works, bondage, and trying endlessly and futilely to please God by the flesh

the mother (v. 26)—Believers are children of the heavenly Jerusalem, the "mother-city" of heaven; in contrast to the slavery of Hagar's children, believers in Christ are free (Gal. 5:1).

children of promise (v. 28)—Just as Isaac inherited the promises made to Abraham, so also are believers the recipients of God's redemptive promises because they are spiritual heirs of Abraham.

he who was born according to the flesh (v. 29)—Ishmael

persecuted him who was born according to the Spirit (v. 29)—Isaac, whom Ishmael mocked at the feast celebrating Isaac's weaning (see Gen. 21:8–9)

Cast out the bondwoman (v. 30)—quoted from Genesis 21:10

Stand fast (5:1)—Stay where you are, Paul asserts, because of the benefit of being free from law and the flesh as a way of salvation and the benefit of the fullness of blessing by grace.

5:1 *Stand fast therefore in the liberty by which Christ has made us free, and do not be entangled again with a yoke of bondage.*

free (5:1)—deliverance from the curse that the law pronounces on the sinner who has been striving unsuccessfully to achieve his own righteousness (Gal. 3:13, 22–26; 4:1–7), but who has now embraced Christ and the salvation granted to him by grace

entangled again (5:1)—better translated "to be burdened by," "to be oppressed by," or "to be subject to," because of its connection with a yoke

yoke of bondage (5:1)—"Yoke" refers to the apparatus used to control a domesticated animal. The Jews referred to the "yoke of the law" as good, the essence of true religion. Paul argued that for those who pursued it as a way of salvation, the law was a yoke of slavery.

1) In speaking of two covenants, how can you be sure that Paul was not contrasting two ways of salvation—one for Old Testament saints and another for New Testament believers?

? ? — one covenant was made w/ the flesh the other through faith.

(Verses to consider: Gal. 2:16; 3:10–14, 21–22)

2) What does Paul say we enjoy as the children of heavenly Jerusalem?

(Verses to consider: Luke 4:18; John 8:36; Rom. 6:18, 22–23; 8:2; 2 Cor. 3:17)

3) What does it mean that, like Isaac, we believers are "children of promise"?

Christ has redeemed us from the lost. We are children of God's promise.

(Verses to consider: Gen. 26:1–3; Eph. 1:3)

GOING DEEPER

For more background on Isaac and Ishmael, the two sons, read Genesis 21:8–20. (See also Genesis 16:1–16; 21:1–7.)

Genesis 21:8–20 (NKJV)

8 So the child grew and was weaned. And Abraham made a great feast on the same day that Isaac was weaned.

9 And Sarah saw the son of Hagar the Egyptian, whom she had borne to Abraham, scoffing.

10 Therefore she said to Abraham, "Cast out this bondwoman and her son; for the son of this bondwoman shall not be heir with my son, namely with Isaac."

11 And the matter was very displeasing in Abraham's sight because of his son.

12 But God said to Abraham, "Do not let it be displeasing in your sight because of the lad or because of your bondwoman. Whatever Sarah has said to you, listen to her voice; for in Isaac your seed shall be called.

13 Yet I will also make a nation of the son of the bondwoman, because he is your seed."

14 So Abraham rose early in the morning, and took bread and a skin of water; and putting it on her shoulder, he gave it and the boy to Hagar, and sent her away. Then she departed and wandered in the Wilderness of Beersheba.

15 And the water in the skin was used up, and she placed the boy under one of the shrubs.

16 Then she went and sat down across from him at a distance of about a bowshot; for she said to herself, "Let me not see the death of the boy." So she sat opposite him, and lifted her voice and wept.

17 And God heard the voice of the lad. Then the angel of God called to Hagar out of heaven, and said to her, "What ails you, Hagar? Fear not, for God has heard the voice of the lad where he is,

18 Arise, lift up the lad and hold him with your hand, for I will make him a great nation."

19 Then God opened her eyes, and she saw a well of water. And she went and filled the skin with water, and gave the lad a drink.

20 So God was with the lad; and he grew and dwelt in the wilderness, and became an archer.

Exploring the Meaning

4) What hints of trouble do you see in the Genesis record of the births and early lives of Ishmael and Isaac?

_____

_____

_____

5) Why did Sarah get upset and send Hagar away (Gen. 12:9–10)?

_____

_____

_____

6) Read 2 Timothy 3:12. What does this verse mean in light of Galatians 4:29, which speaks of ancient and present persecution? How would you explain these verses to someone unfamiliar with the Bible?

_____

_____

_____

(Verses to consider: Matt. 10:22–25; John 16:2, 33; 1 Pet. 4:12–14)

7) Read 2 Thessalonians 1:9. What does this verse say about the destiny of those who attempt to be justified on the basis of keeping the law?

_____

_____

_____

(Verses to consider: Matt. 8:12; 22:12–13; 25:30; Luke 13:28)

Truth for Today

Galatians 4:21–5:1 is an extended series of contrasts between the way of law and the way of grace, the way of works and the way of faith, the way of man and the way of God. Following that same pattern, we also explicitly or implicitly see the contrasts of Hagar/Sarah, Ishmael/Isaac, children of Satan/children of God, commandments/promise, wrath/mercy, bondage/freedom, old covenant/new covenant, Sinai/Zion, present Jerusalem/Jerusalem above, fleshly/spiritual, rejection/inheritance, and lostness/salvation. Throughout this letter, and indeed throughout all of Scripture, such contrasts reflect and demonstrate the contrast of the ages: the way of Satan and the way of God. But in God's ultimate and unchangeable plan, Satan and his way will be destroyed, and only the way of God will remain, forever and ever. Vacillating between the two is unacceptable.

REFLECTING ON THE TEXT

8) This passage speaks of heaven (that is, "the Jerusalem above"). How does the hope of heaven change the way you live now?

_____

_____

_____

_____

9) Paul reminds us to stand fast in the "liberty" we have in Christ. What are some ways you can enjoy the freedom you have in Christ—in your relationships, in your attitudes, in your behavior?

_____

_____

_____

_____

10) In what ways do you think and act as though your salvation depends on earning God's approval through your actions rather than God's grace alone? What would it look like for you to "not be entangled again with a yoke of bondage"? In other words, what specific changes do you need to make in your life?

_____

_____

_____

_____

_____

PERSONAL RESPONSE

Write out additional reflections, questions you may have, or a prayer.

_____

_____

_____

_____

_____

_____

_____

_____

_____

_____

_____

_____

_____

_____

_____

_____

_____

_____

_____

_____

_____

_____

_____

_____

10

CALLED TO FREEDOM
Galatians 5:2–15

DRAWING NEAR

You are leading a Bible study and the conversation turns to the subject of Christian freedom. This precipitates a testy exchange between one member who tends to be a bit legalistic and another attendee who participates in many "questionable" behaviors without a seeming twinge of conscience. What do you say?

_____

_____

_____

Over and over the New Testament calls believers to serve one another. How would you grade yourself in the area of service? Why?

_____

_____

_____

THE CONTEXT

After defending his apostleship and his message of justification by faith, Paul next applied that doctrine to practical Christian living, emphasizing that right doctrine should result in right living. His contention is that sanctification should result from justification. The life of genuine faith is more than belief in divine truth; it is also the bearing of divine fruit.

The freedom for which Christ sets us free is the freedom to live a life of righteousness in the power of the Holy Spirit. God's standard of holiness has not changed. As Jesus makes clear in the Sermon on the Mount, it requires not simply outward performance but inner perfection. Through His Holy Spirit, believers have the ability to live internal lives of righteousness.

The final two chapters are a portrait of the Spirit-filled life, of the believer's implementing the life of faith under the control and in the energy of the Holy Spirit. The Spirit-filled life thereby becomes in itself a powerful testimony to the power of justification by faith. In making his appeal for living the Spirit-filled life of freedom, he explained freedom's grand nature and purpose.

KEYS TO THE TEXT

Circumcision: Most Jews in New Testament times firmly believed that circumcision not only set them apart from all other men as God's chosen people but also made them acceptable to God. Because these beliefs were strongly held in Judaism, Jewish converts in the early church carried many of them over into Christianity. Circumcision and following the law of Moses became such divisive issues that the apostles and elders called a special council in Jerusalem to settle the matter. They unanimously decided, and expressed in a letter sent to all the churches, that obedience to Mosaic ritual, including circumcision, was not necessary for salvation (see Acts 15:19–29). Paul objected to the notion that circumcision had some spiritual benefit or merit with God and was a prerequisite or necessary component of salvation. Circumcision had meaning in Israel when it was a physical symbol of a cleansed heart (see Jer. 9:24–26) and served as a reminder of God's covenant of salvation promise (Gen. 17:9–10). A person who trusts in circumcision, or in any other ceremony or work, nullifies the work of Christ on his behalf. He places himself under the law, and a person under the law must obey it with absolute perfection, which is humanly impossible. "For in Christ Jesus neither circumcision nor uncircumcision avails anything, but faith working through love" (Gal. 5:6).

UNLEASHING THE TEXT

Read 5:2–15, noting the key words and definitions next to the passage.

Christ . . . profit you nothing (v. 2)—The atoning sacrifice of Christ cannot benefit anyone who trusts in law and ceremony for salvation.

a debtor to keep the whole law (v. 3)—God's standard is perfect righteousness, and thus a failure to keep only one part of the law falls short of the standard.

estranged from Christ . . . fallen from grace (v. 4)—The Greek word for "estranged" means "to be separated" or "to be severed." The word for "fallen" means "to lose one's grasp on something." Paul's clear meaning is that any attempt to be justified by the law is to reject salvation by grace alone through faith alone. Those once exposed to the gracious truth of the gospel who then turn their backs on Christ and seek to be justified by the law are separated from Christ and lose all prospects of God's gracious salvation. Their desertion of Christ and the gospel proves that their faith was never genuine.

Galatians 5:2–15 (NKJV)

2 *Indeed I, Paul, say to you that if you become circumcised, Christ will profit you nothing.*

3 *And I testify again to every man who becomes circumcised that he is a debtor to keep the whole law.*

4 *You have become estranged from Christ, you who attempt to be justified by law; you have fallen from grace.*

5 *For we through the Spirit eagerly wait for the hope of righteousness by faith.*

6 *For in Christ Jesus neither circumcision nor uncircumcision avails anything, but faith working through love.* ✻

7 *You ran well. Who hindered you from obeying the truth?*

8 *This persuasion does not come from Him who calls you.*

9 *A little leaven leavens the whole lump.*

10 *I have confidence in you, in the Lord, that you will have no other mind; but he who troubles you shall bear his judgment, whoever he is.*

11 *And I, brethren, if I still preach circumcision, why do I still suffer persecution? Then the offense of the cross has ceased.*

12 *I could wish that those who trouble you would even cut themselves off!*

the hope of righteousness by faith (v. 5)—Christians already possess the imputed righteousness of Christ, but they still await the completed and perfected righteousness that is yet to come at glorification.

neither circumcision nor uncircumcision avails anything (v. 6)—Nothing done or not done in the flesh, even religious ceremony, makes any difference in one's relationship to God. What is external is immaterial and worthless, unless it reflects genuine internal righteousness.

faith working through love (v. 6)—Saving faith proves its genuine character by works of love; the one who lives by faith is internally motivated by love for God and Christ, which supernaturally issues forth in reverent worship, genuine obedience, and self-sacrificing love for others.

You ran well (v. 7)—Paul compares the Galatians' life of faith with a race. They had a good beginning—they had received the gospel message by faith and had begun to live their Christian lives by faith as well.

obeying the truth (v. 7)—a reference to believers' true way of living, including both their response to the true gospel in salvation (see Acts 6:7; Rom. 2:8; 6:17; 2 Thess. 1:8) and their consequent response to obey the Word of God in sanctification. Paul wrote more about salvation and sanctification being a matter of obedience in Romans 1:5; 6:16–17; 16:26. The legalistic influence of the Judaizers prevented the unsaved from responding in faith to the gospel of grace and true believers from living by faith.

This persuasion (v. 8)—salvation by works. God does not promote legalism; any doctrine that claims His gracious work is insufficient to save is false.

leaven (v. 9)—a common axiomatic saying (see 1 Cor. 5:6) regarding the influence of yeast in dough. Leaven is often used in Scripture to denote sin (Matt. 16:6, 12) because of its permeating power.

confidence in you (v. 10)—Paul expresses encouraging assurance that the Lord will be faithful to keep His own from falling into gross heresy; they will persevere and be preserved (Jude 24).

judgment (v. 10)—All false teachers will incur strict and devastating eternal condemnation.

still preach circumcision (v. 11)—Apparently the Judaizers had falsely claimed that Paul agreed with their teaching; he makes the point, however, that if he was preaching circumcision as necessary for salvation, why were the Judaizers persecuting him instead of supporting him?

offense of the cross (v. 11)—The Greek word for "offense" can mean "trap," "snare," or "stumbling block." Any offer of salvation that strips a person of the opportunity to earn it by his own merit breeds opposition (see Rom. 9:33).

cut themselves off (v. 12)—Better translated "mutilate themselves," the Greek word was often used of castration, such as in the cult of Cybele, whose priests were self-made eunuchs. Paul's ironic point is that since the Judaizers were so insistent on circumcision as a means of pleasing God, they should go to the extreme of religious devotion and mutilate themselves.

opportunity for the flesh (v. 13)—The Greek word for "opportunity" was often used to refer to a central base of military operations (see Rom. 7:8). In the context, "flesh" refers to the sinful inclinations of fallen humanity; the freedom Christians have is not a base from which they can sin freely and without consequence.

13 *For you, brethren, have been called to liberty; only do not use liberty as an opportunity for the flesh, but through love serve one another.*

14 *For all the law is fulfilled in one word, even in this: "You shall love your neighbor as yourself."*

15 *But if you bite and devour one another, beware lest you be consumed by one another!*

serve one another (v. 13)—Christian freedom is not for selfish fulfillment but for serving others.

all the law (v. 14)—The ethics of the former Old Testament law are the same as those of the New Testament gospel, as indicated in the quote from Leviticus 19:18. When a Christian genuinely loves others, he or she fulfills all the moral requirements of the former Mosaic Law concerning them; this is the ruling principle of Christian freedom (Gal. 5:6, 13).

bite and devour one another (v. 15)—The imagery is of wild animals savagely attacking and killing each other—a graphic picture of what happens in the spiritual realm when believers do not love and serve each other.

1) Did Paul view circumcision as an inherently bad practice? How do you know? (See 5:6) What did Paul see as the more important issue instead?

No - but reversed for as an expression of God.

(Verses to consider: Deut. 30:6; Jer. 4:4; Acts 16:1–3; Phil. 3:3–5)

2) What did Paul mean when he said that the Galatians "ran well"? What caused them to stumble in their race?

Some other influences caused them to stumble.

(Verses to consider: 1 Cor. 9:24–27)

94

3) According to Paul, how do liberty and love work together? What should liberty produce?

faithfullness hope and righteousness

4) How does Paul summarize the law (v. 14)? Whose words is he echoing? What point does he make with this quote?

(Verses to consider: Matt. 22:36–40; Rom. 7:12; 8:4; James 2:8–10)

GOING DEEPER

Paul addresses the issue of Christian liberty in many areas of life. Read Romans 14:1–15 for further insight.

Romans 14:1–15 (NKJV)

1 *Receive one who is weak in the faith, but not to disputes over doubtful things.*

2 *For one believes he may eat all things, but he who is weak eats only vegetables.*

3 *Let not him who eats despise him who does not eat, and let not him who does not eat judge him who eats; for God has received him.*

4 *Who are you to judge another's servant? To his own master he stands or falls. Indeed, he will be made to stand, for God is able to make him stand.*

5 *One person esteems one day above another; another esteems every day alike. Let each be fully convinced in his own mind.*

6 *He who observes the day, observes it to the Lord; and he who does not observe the day, to the Lord he does not observe it. He who eats, eats to the Lord, for he gives God thanks; and he who does not eat, to the Lord he does not eat, and gives God thanks.*

7 *For none of us lives to himself, and no one dies to himself.*

8 *For if we live, we live to the Lord; and if we die, we die to the Lord. Therefore, whether we live or die, we are the Lord's.*

9 *For to this end Christ died and rose and lived again, that He might be Lord of both the dead and the living.*

10 *But why do you judge your brother? Or why do you show contempt for your brother? For we shall all stand before the judgment seat of Christ.*

11 *For it is written: "'As I live,' says the LORD, 'Every knee shall bow to Me, and every tongue shall confess to God.'"*

12 *So then each of us shall give account of himself to God.*

13 *Therefore let us not judge one another anymore, but rather resolve this, not to put a stumbling block or a cause to fall in our brother's way.*

14 *I know and am convinced by the Lord Jesus that there is nothing unclean of itself; but to him who considers anything to be unclean, to him it is unclean.*

15 *Yet if your brother is grieved because of your food, you are no longer walking in love. Do not destroy with your food the one for whom Christ died.*

EXPLORING THE MEANING

5) According to this passage, what is the guiding rule for Christian freedom?

Not to put a stumbling block in the way of your brother.

6) Read 1 John 2:19. How does this passage address the idea of deserting Christ and the gospel that Paul discusses in Galatians 5:4?

If they were part of us, they would have stayed. True brothers stick together out of love.

(Verses to consider: Luke 8:13–14; Heb. 6:4–6)

7) Read Romans 2:25–29. How does this passage contribute to Paul's argument in Galatians 5:5–6 that external religious actions are meaningless without an internal change?

validates that we need circumcision of the heart.

TRUTH FOR TODAY

Someone has pictured legalism and libertinism as two parallel streams that run between earth and heaven. The stream of legalism is clear, sparkling, and pure; but its waters run so deep and furiously that no one can enter it without being drowned or smashed on the rocks of its harsh demands. The stream of libertinism, by contrast, is relatively quiet and still, and crossing it seems easy and attractive. But its waters are so contaminated with poisons and pollutants that to try to cross it is also certain death. Both streams are uncrossable and deadly, one because of impossible moral and spiritual demands, the other because of moral and spiritual filth. But spanning those two deadly streams is the bridge of the gospel of Jesus Christ, the only passage from earth to heaven. The two streams lead to death because they are man's ways. The gospel leads to life because it is God's way.

REFLECTING ON THE TEXT

8) The line between legalism and libertinism is often fuzzy. Which "stream" do you tend to follow in your life—rigidly following the "rules" of Christianity, or freely doing what you want without regard for how it affects others?

The stream of libertinism

9) This lesson speaks of the importance of "faith working through love." What areas in your life need to demonstrate more evidence of a loving faith?

As a father loving spirit.

10) If Paul were to write a letter to you personally, would he say that you are "running well"? Why?

He'd say, I'm running. but not well. Getting tripped up frequently.

Personal Response

Write out additional reflections, questions you may have, or a prayer.

_____

_____

_____

_____

_____

_____

_____

_____

_____

_____

_____

_____

_____

_____

_____

_____

_____

_____

_____

_____

_____

_____

_____

11

WALKING IN THE SPIRIT
Galatians 5:16–26

DRAWING NEAR

What do you think of the following statements as summaries of the Christian life? Are they biblical phrases or not?

- "Let go and let God!"
- "It's all of Him, and none of us."
- "Keep seeking more of the Spirit's anointings, new out-pourings."
- "Surrender completely to Jesus."
- "Be sold out to Christ."
- "Fight the good fight and run the race!"
- "Practice the presence of God."

Yes because they focus on grace & faith. But never said "done."

How would *you* summarize how to live the Christian life?

When you think of the Holy Spirit, what comes to mind?

Peace & Surrender,

THE CONTEXT

The final two chapters of Galatians provide a practical guidebook to how the gracious gospel should make a difference in a Christian's everyday life. Just as Jesus Christ is the primary Person behind justification, the Holy Spirit is the primary Person behind sanctification—becoming holy. Believers can no more sanctify themselves than they can save themselves in the first place.

In its most profound yet simple definition, the faithful Christian life is lived under the direction and by the power of the Spirit. That is the theme of 5:16–25, which tells believers to "walk by the Spirit" and to be "led by the Spirit." In short, Paul's argument is that the Holy Spirit makes the life of faith work. Were it not for the indwelling power of the Holy Spirit, the life of faith would be no more spiritually productive or acceptable to God than the life of law.

KEYS TO THE TEXT

Walk in the Spirit: All believers have the presence of the indwelling Holy Spirit, the third person of the Trinity (see Rom. 8:9; 1 Cor. 6:19–20), as their personal source of power for living to please God. The form of the Greek verb translated "walk" indicates continuous action, or a habitual lifestyle. Walking also implies progress; as a believer submits to the Spirit's control—that is, responds in obedience to the simple commands of Scripture—he or she grows in his or her spiritual life. The Holy Spirit produces fruit, which consists of nine characteristics or attitudes that are inextricably linked with each other and are commanded of believers throughout the New Testament.

UNLEASHING THE TEXT

Read 5:16–26, noting the key words and definitions next to the passage.

Galatians 5:16–26 (NKJV)

the flesh (v. 16)—This is not simply the physical body. It includes the mind, will, and emotions, which are all subject to sin, and refers, in general to our unredeemed humanness.

contrary to one another (v. 17)—The flesh opposes the work of the Spirit and leads the believer toward sinful behavior that he or she would not otherwise be compelled to do.

led by the Spirit . . . not under the law (v. 18)—Take your

16 *I say then: Walk in the Spirit, and you shall not fulfill the lust of the flesh.*

17 *For the flesh lusts against the Spirit, and the Spirit against the flesh; and these are contrary to one another, so that you do not do the things that you wish.*

18 *But if you are led by the Spirit, you are not under the law.*

19 *Now the works of the flesh are evident, which are: adultery, fornication, uncleanness, lewdness,*

choice; these are mutually exclusive. Either you live by the power of the Holy Spirit, which results in righteous behavior and spiritual attitudes (Gal. 3:22–29), or you live by the law, which can only produce unrighteous behavior and attitudes (vv. 19–21).

now the works of the flesh . . . (vv. 19–21)—These sins characterize all unredeemed humankind, though not every person manifests all these sins nor exhibits them to the same degree. Paul's list, which is not exhaustive, encompasses three areas of human life: sex, religion, and human relationships.

evident (v. 19)—The flesh manifests itself in obvious and certain ways.

20 *idolatry, sorcery, hatred, contentions, jealousies,*
outbursts of wrath, selfish ambitions, dissensions,
heresies,

21 *envy, murders, drunkenness, revelries, and the like;*
of which I tell you beforehand, just as I also told you
in time past, that those who practice such things
will not inherit the kingdom of God.

22 *But the fruit of the Spirit is love, joy, peace,*
longsuffering, kindness, goodness, faithfulness,

fornication (v. 19)—The Greek word is *porneia*, from which the English word "pornography" comes. It refers to all illicit sexual activity, including (but not limited to) adultery, premarital sex, homosexuality, bestiality, incest, and prostitution.

lewdness (v. 19)—The word originally referred to any excessive behavior or lack of restraint, but eventually became associated with sexual excess and indulgence.

sorcery (v. 20)—This Greek word, from which our English word "pharmacy" comes, originally referred to medicines in general but eventually only to mood- and mind-altering drugs, as well as the occult, witchcraft, and magic. Many pagan religious practices required the use of these drugs to aid in the communication with deities.

contentions . . . heresies (v. 20)—Many of these sins manifested in the area of human relationships have to do with some form of anger: "Hatred" results in "contentions" (strife); "jealousies" (hateful resentment) result in "outbursts of wrath" (sudden, unrestrained expressions of hostility); the next four represent animosity between individuals and groups.

drunkenness, revelries (v. 21)—probably a specific reference to the orgies that characterized pagan, idolatrous worship; generally, it refers to all rowdy, boisterous, and crude behavior.

practice (v. 21)—Here is the key word in Paul's warning; the sense of this Greek verb describes continual, habitual action. Although believers undoubtedly can commit these sins, those people whose basic character is summed up in the uninterrupted and unrepentant practice of them cannot belong to God.

will not inherit the kingdom of God (v. 21)—The unregenerate are barred from entering the spiritual kingdom of redeemed people over whom Christ now rules, and they will be excluded from His millennial kingdom and the eternal state of blessing that follows it.

love (v. 22)—One of several Greek words for love, *agape*, refers to the love of choice, not an emotional affection, physical attraction, or a familial bond, but the respect, devotion, and affection that lead to willing, self-sacrificial service.

joy (v. 22)—a happiness based on unchanging divine promises and eternal spiritual realities. It is the sense of well-being experienced by one who knows all is well between himself or herself and the Lord; it is not the result of favorable circumstances, and even occurs when those circumstances are the most painful and severe. Joy is a gift from God, and as such, believers are not to manufacture it but to delight in the blessing they already possess.

peace (v. 22)—the inner calm that results from confidence in one's saving relationship with Christ. The verb form denotes binding together and is reflected in the expression "having it all together"; like joy, peace is not related to one's circumstances (John 14:27; Rom. 8:28; Phil. 4:6-7, 9).

longsuffering (v. 22)—the patience to endure injuries inflicted by others and the willingness to accept irritating or painful situations (Eph. 4:2; Col. 3:12; 1 Tim. 1:15-16)

kindness (v. 22)—tender concern for others, reflected in a desire to treat others gently, just as the Lord treats all believers (Matt. 11:28, 29; 19:13-14; 2 Tim. 2:24)

goodness (v. 22)—moral and spiritual excellence manifested in active kindness (Rom. 5:7); believers are commanded to exemplify goodness (6:10; 2 Thess. 1:11).

faithfulness (v. 22)—loyalty and trustworthiness (Lam. 3:22; Phil. 2:7-9; 1 Thess. 5:24; Rev. 2:10)

gentleness (v. 23)—Better translated "meekness," this is a humble and gentle attitude that is patiently submissive in every offense, while having no desire for revenge or retribution. In the New Testament, it is used to describe three attitudes: submission to the will of God (Col. 3:12), teachability (James 1:21), and consideration of others (Eph. 4:2).

23 *gentleness, self-control. Against such there is no law.*

24 *And those who are Christ's have crucified the flesh with its passions and desires.*

25 *If we live in the Spirit, let us also walk in the Spirit.*

26 *Let us not become conceited, provoking one another, envying one another.*

self-control (v. 23)—This refers to restraining passions and appetites (1 Cor. 9:25; 2 Pet. 1:5–6).

no law (v. 23)—When a Christian walks by the Spirit and manifests His fruit, he or she needs no external law to produce the attitudes and behavior that please God (see Rom. 8:4).

have crucified the flesh (v. 24)—one of four uses of "crucified" that does not refer to Christ's crucifixion. Paul states that the flesh has been executed, yet the spiritual battle still rages in the believer (Rom. 7:14–25). Paul's use looks back to the cross of Christ, where the death of the flesh and its power to reign over believers was actually accomplished (Rom. 6:1–11). Christians must wait until their glorification before they are finally rid of their unredeemed humanness (Rom. 8:23), yet by walking in the Spirit they can please God in this world.

1) Paul contrasts the works of the flesh with the fruit of the Spirit. Is he arguing that those who commit these sins prove they are not really Christians? Why or why not? What Scripture would you use to support your answer?

_____

_____

_____

_____

_____

2) What results when we live in the power of our flesh? On the other hand, what happens when we live by faith in the power of the Spirit?

_____

_____

_____

_____

_____

3) After describing the fruit of the Spirit, Paul says that "against such there is no law." What does he mean by that?

_____

_____

_____

_____

_____

_____

(Verse to consider: Rom. 8:4)

GOING DEEPER

For more insight about what it means to walk in the Spirit, read Ephesians 5:1–16.

Ephesians 5:1–16 (NKJV)

1   *Therefore be imitators of God as dear children.*
2   *And walk in love, as Christ also has loved us and given Himself for us, an offering and a sacrifice to God for a sweet-smelling aroma.*
3   *But fornication and all uncleanness or covetousness, let it not even be named among you, as is fitting for saints;*
4   *neither filthiness, nor foolish talking, nor coarse jesting, which are not fitting, but rather giving of thanks.*
5   *For this you know, that no fornicator, unclean person, nor covetous man, who is an idolater, has any inheritance in the kingdom of Christ and God.*
6   *Let no one deceive you with empty words, for because of these things the wrath of God comes upon the sons of disobedience.*
7   *Therefore do not be partakers with them.*
8   *For you were once darkness, but now you are light in the Lord. Walk as children of light*
9   *(for the fruit of the Spirit is in all goodness, righteousness, and truth),*
10 *finding out what is acceptable to the Lord.*
11 *And have no fellowship with the unfruitful works of darkness, but rather expose them.*
12 *For it is shameful even to speak of those things which are done by them in secret.*
13 *But all things that are exposed are made manifest by the light, for whatever makes manifest is light.*

14 *Therefore He says: "Awake, you who sleep, Arise from the dead, And Christ will give you light."*

15 *See then that you walk circumspectly, not as fools but as wise,*

16 *redeeming the time, because the days are evil.*

EXPLORING THE MEANING

4) How does the list of works of darkness in Ephesians compare with Paul's list of fleshly activities in Galatians 5 (vv. 3–6)?

_____

_____

_____

_____

_____

5) What light do these verses shed on the idea of walking by the Spirit (vv. 8–15)?

_____

_____

_____

_____

_____

_____

(Verses to consider: Rom. 8:13; Col. 3:16)

6) Read Romans 6:6. What does it mean that our flesh has been crucified?

_____

_____

_____

_____

_____

(Verses to consider: Rom. 6:7–14)

TRUTH FOR TODAY

Because believers have new life in Jesus Christ, they should also have a new way of life. The Spirit never fails to produce some fruit in a believer's life, but the Lord desires "much fruit" (John 15:8). As an unredeemed person, possessing only a fallen, sinful nature will inevitably manifest that nature in "the deeds of the flesh" (v. 19), so a believer, possessing a redeemed new nature will inevitably manifest that new nature in the fruit of the Spirit. But it is always possible for the believer to bear and manifest more fruit if he is receptive to the Spirit. The Spirit's provision of fruit might be compared to a man standing on a ladder in an orchard, picking the fruit and dropping it into a basket held by a helper below. No matter how much fruit is picked and dropped, the helper will not receive any unless he is standing under the ladder with his basket ready.

REFLECTING ON THE TEXT

7) Many followers of Jesus look for and pursue a dramatic experience or sudden insight that they think will help them attain spiritual maturity and consistency. Based on your study in this lesson, why is this an erroneous understanding of the Christian life?

_____

_____

_____

_____

_____

_____

8) How would you describe/define "the flesh"? In what specific areas does your flesh seem to rear its ugly head most often?

_____

_____

_____

_____

_____

_____

9) How do you know when you are walking in the Spirit? Is there a way to know for sure?

_____

_____

_____

_____

_____

_____

_____

_____

_____

10) If a young Christian came to you and said, "I don't see much of the fruit of the Spirit in my life," what counsel would you give?

_____

_____

_____

_____

_____

_____

_____

_____

_____

_____

_____

_____

PERSONAL RESPONSE

Write out additional reflections, questions you may have, or a prayer.

_____

_____

_____

_____

_____

_____

_____

_____

_____

_____

_____

_____

_____

_____

_____

_____

_____

_____

_____

_____

_____

_____

Additional Notes

12

A GRACE-FILLED LIFE
Galatians 6:1–18

DRAWING NEAR

In this closing section, Paul speaks about correcting a Christian brother or sister. Have you ever been gently confronted about sin in your life by another believer? What happened?

Yes. After giving this brother permission to correct me. I told one accordable. It was a loving but direct correction.

What new things have you learned about God in this study of Galatians? About yourself?

I have faith to focus on the fruit of the spirit. Be gentle and loving. Don't be critical. And be sensitive to issues that others struggle over

If you had to tell someone what salvation by grace is all about, how would you explain it?

Explain it as a gift. Something that is not earned. I know it would be hard to explain and easier to demonstrate through a relationship.

THE CONTEXT

The end of Paul's letter to the Galatian churches carries the same weight of seriousness and urgency as the rest of it. Both the beginning and end (1:3; 6:18) commend readers to God's grace and express Paul's deep concern for the spiritual welfare of those to whom he was writing. But Paul took no time for the personal amenities found in most of his other letters. It is almost as if the courier were standing at the door, waiting for Paul to finish writing so he could rush the letter on its way.

Following brief instructions about restoring a sinning brother and the inviolable spiritual law of sowing and reaping, Paul contrasted those who would glory in the flesh with those who glory only in the cross. Except for the closing

109

benediction (v. 18), verses 11 to the end are largely a parting salvo against the Judaizers, whose heretical activities prompted the letter in the first place. They were teaching the spurious, human-made gospel of salvation by works and of living under the government of law, in complete contradiction to the divine gospel of salvation by grace and living by the Spirit that Paul had preached when he ministered in Galatia. Paul condemned their motives for teaching their legalistic perversion of the gospel, declaring that they were motivated by religious pride, by cowardice, and by hypocrisy.

Paul, on the other hand, gloried in the cross because it was this sacrifice of the Lord Jesus Christ that was the source of his and every believer's righteousness and acceptance before God. Only the cross is able to bring an end to humankind's hopeless frustration in pursuing God through works.

KEYS TO THE TEXT

Reaping and Sowing: In its literal, physical sense, that rudimentary law of agriculture—you reap what you sow—is self-evident. Absolutely universal, it applies equally to every farmer and gardener in every time and place—to the young and the old, the experienced and the inexperienced, the wise and the foolish, the saved and the unsaved. This law operates the same no matter who plants the seeds. It is as impartial, predictable, and immutable as the law of gravity. And although men's sin and self-deception often prevent them from seeing or acknowledging it, the principle holds just as true in the moral and spiritual realms. God's Word is clear. The wicked "sow the wind, and they reap the whirlwind," whereas those who "sow with a view to righteousness, reap in accordance with kindness" (Hos. 8:7; 10:12).

The Cross: Paul gloried in the cross because Christ's sacrifice on the cross is the source of his and every believer's righteousness and acceptance before God—bringing an end to the hopeless frustration of pursuing God through works. God "made Him who knew no sin to be sin on our behalf that we might become the righteousness of God in Him" (2 Cor. 5:21). Christians honor and praise the cross because Christ's sacrifice there provided redemption and eternal life, making the cross the supreme symbol of the gospel, the religion of divine accomplishment.

UNLEASHING THE TEXT

Read 6:1–18, noting the key words and definitions next to the passage.

Galatians 6:1–18 (NKJV)

1 Brethren, if a man is overtaken in any trespass, you who are spiritual restore such a one in a spirit of gentleness, considering yourself lest you also be tempted.

2 Bear one another's burdens, and so fulfill the law of Christ.

3 For if anyone thinks himself to be something, when he is nothing, he deceives himself.

4 But let each one examine his own work, and then he will have rejoicing in himself alone, and not in another.

5 For each one shall bear his own load.

6 Let him who is taught the word share in all good things with him who teaches.

7 Do not be deceived, God is not mocked; for whatever a man sows, that he will also reap.

8 For he who sows to his flesh will of the flesh reap corruption, but he who sows to the Spirit will of the Spirit reap everlasting life.

overtaken (v. 1)—literally "caught," which may imply the person was actually seen committing the sin, or that he was caught or snared by the sin itself

you . . . spiritual (v. 1)—those believers who are walking in the Spirit, filled with the Spirit and evidencing the fruit of the Spirit (Gal. 5:22–23)

restore (v. 1)—Sometimes used metaphorically for settling disputes or arguments, it literally means "to mend" or "repair," and was used of setting a broken bone or repairing a dislocated limb. The basic process of restoration is outlined in Matthew 18:15–20.

considering (v. 1)—also "looking to, observing"; the Greek form strongly emphasizes a continual, diligent attentiveness

Bear one another's burdens (v. 2)—"Burdens" are extra heavy loads, which here represent difficulties or problems people have trouble dealing with. "Bear" connotes carrying something with endurance.

the law of Christ (v. 2)—the law of love which fulfills the entire law

examine (v. 4)—literally "to approve something after testing it"; believers first must be sure their lives are right with God before giving spiritual help to others

have rejoicing in himself (v. 4)—Believers should rejoice or boast in the Lord only for what God has done in him or her (see 2 Cor. 10:12–18), not for what he or she supposedly has accomplished compared to other believers.

bear his own load (v. 5)—This is not a contradiction to verse 2. "Load" has no connotation of difficulty; it refers to life's routine obligations and each believer's ministry calling. God requires faithfulness in meeting those responsibilities.

all good things (v. 6)—Although this expression could refer to material compensation, the context suggests that Paul is referring to the spiritually and morally excellent things learned from the Word, in which they fellowship together. Paul uses this same term to describe the gospel (Rom. 10:15).

sows to his flesh (v. 8)—Here it means pandering to the flesh's evil desires.

corruption (v. 8)—from the Greek word for degeneration, as in decaying food; sin always corrupts and, when left unchecked, always makes a person progressively worse in character (see Rom. 6:23)

sows to the Spirit (v. 8)—to walk by the Holy Spirit

everlasting life (v. 8)—This expression describes not only a life that endures forever but, primarily, the highest quality of living that one can experience (see Eph. 1:3, 18).

opportunity (v. 10)—The Greek word is *kairos* and refers to a distinct, fixed time period, rather than occasional moments. Paul's point is that the believer's entire life provides the unique privilege by which he or she can serve others in Christ's name.

especially . . . the household of faith (v. 10)—Our love for fellow Christians is the primary test of our love for God.

with what large letters (v. 11)—This can be interpreted in two ways: (1) Paul's poor eyesight forced him to use large letters (Gal. 4:13, 15); or (2) instead of the normal cursive style of writing used by professional scribes, Paul used the large, block letters (frequently employed in public notices) to emphasize the letter's content rather than its form. It was a visible picture that contrasted his concern

9 *And let us not grow weary while doing good, for in due season we shall reap if we do not lose heart.*

10 *Therefore, as we have opportunity, let us do good to all, especially to those who are of the household of faith.*

11 *See with what large letters I have written to you with my own hand!*

12 *As many as desire to make a good showing in the flesh, these would compel you to be circumcised, only that they may not suffer persecution for the cross of Christ.*

13 *For not even those who are circumcised keep the law, but they desire to have you circumcised that they may boast in your flesh.*

14 *But God forbid that I should boast except in the cross of our Lord Jesus Christ, by whom the world has been crucified to me, and I to the world.*

with the content of the gospel for the Judaizers' only concern: appearances. The expression served as a transition to his concluding remarks.

I have written . . . my own hand (v. 11)—As a good translation of the Greek verb, this indicates that Paul wrote the entire letter by his own hand, not merely penning a brief statement at the end of dictation to a secretary as he did other times (see 1 Cor. 16:21; 2 Thess. 3:17). Paul wrote this letter himself to make sure the Galatians knew he—not some forger—was writing it and to personalize the document, given the importance and severity of its contents.

good showing (v. 12)—The Judaizers were motivated by religious pride and wanted to impress others with their external piety (see Matt. 6:1–7).

may not suffer persecution (v. 12)—The Judaizers were more concerned about their personal safety than correct doctrine. By adhering more to the Mosaic Law than to the gospel of Jesus, they hoped to avoid social and financial ostracism from other Jews and maintain their protected status as Jews within the Roman Empire.

circumcised (v. 13)—specifically, in this case, the Judaizers (see Acts 11:2)

boast in your flesh (v. 13)—They zealously worked to win Gentile converts to the law so they could brag about their effective proselytizing.

boast except in the cross (v. 14)—The Greek word for "boast" is a basic expression of praise, unlike the English word, which necessarily includes the aspect of pride. Paul glories and rejoices in the sacrifice of Jesus Christ.

the world (v. 14)—the evil, Satanic system

crucified to me, and I to the world (v. 14)—The world is spiritually dead to believers, and they are dead to the world.

15 *For in Christ Jesus neither circumcision nor uncircumcision avails anything, but a new creation.*

16 *And as many as walk according to this rule, peace and mercy be upon them, and upon the Israel of God.*

17 *From now on let no one trouble me, for I bear in my body the marks of the Lord Jesus.*

18 *Brethren, the grace of our Lord Jesus Christ be with your spirit. Amen.*

a new creation (v. 15)—the new birth

peace and mercy (v. 16)—the results of salvation: "peace" is the believer's new relationship to God (Rom. 5:1; 8:6; Col. 3:15), and "mercy" is the forgiveness of all his sins and the setting aside of God's judgment (Ps. 25:6; Dan. 9:18; Matt. 5:7; Luke 1:50; Rom. 12:1; Eph. 2:4; Titus 3:5)

Israel of God (v. 16)—all Jewish believers in Christ, that is, those who are both physical and spiritual descendants of Abraham (see Rom. 2:28–29; 9:6–7; Gal. 3:7, 18)

marks (v. 17)—the physical results of persecution (scars, wounds, etc.) that identified Paul as one who had suffered for the Lord (see Acts 16:22; 2 Cor. 1:5; 4:10; Col. 1:24)

1) What is involved in restoring a Christian brother or sister who has sinned?

Patience and prayer, Self-examination loving kindness, Concern and Compassion

(Verses to consider: Matt. 7:3–5; 18:15–17; Rom. 15:1–2; 1 Thess. 5:14; Heb. 12:3–11)

2) What does Paul mean when he commands each believer to "bear his own load"?

Focus on your own actions first. Not be critical of others

3) How would you explain the law of sowing and reaping to a child?

You get your reward based on what you put into it. You do bad you'll get bad back. Do good and you'll get good in return.

(Verses to consider: Job 4:8; Prov. 1:31–33; Hos. 10:12)

4) What was Paul's point in his contrast of boasting in the flesh with boasting in the cross?

- Boasting about your accomplish[ments]
  you are the center
- Boasting in the cross. boasting
  in Christs accomplishments.

(Verses to consider: Rom. 8:1–3; 1 Cor. 2:2; 1 Pet. 2:24)

Going Deeper

For more about reaping and sowing in the sinful nature and in the Spirit, read Romans 8:5–9:

Romans 8:5–9 (NKJV)

5 *For those who live according to the flesh set their minds on the things of the flesh, but those who live according to the Spirit, the things of the Spirit.*
6 *For to be carnally minded is death, but to be spiritually minded is life and peace.*
7 *Because the carnal mind is enmity against God; for it is not subject to the law of God, nor indeed can be.*
8 *So then, those who are in the flesh cannot please God.*
9 *But you are not in the flesh but in the Spirit, if indeed the Spirit of God dwells in you. Now if anyone does not have the Spirit of Christ, he is not His.*

Exploring the Meaning

5) What evidence will there be in our lives if we are sowing to please the Spirit? What fruit will we reap?

Joy, peace, loving, kindness
seems too simple. How do
we know we are definitively
in the spirit.
I feel I am in the flesh
99.9% of the time.

114

6) Read John 13:34–35. Why is demonstrating love for fellow Christians so important?

If we love one another they will know we are disciples of Christ.

✗ Our love for one another is a major witness

(Verses to consider: Rom. 12:10–13; 1 John 4:20–21)

7) Read 1 John 2:15–16 and Galatians 2:20. Describe what a true believer's relationship with the world will look like.

The true believer is not ✗ impacted by the things of this world. These things just bounce off like a bell.

(Verses to consider: Rom. 6:2–10; Phil. 3:20–21 1 John 5:4–5)

Wul in 6th person

God installs the blinders. See Jun 5:4-5

TRUTH FOR TODAY

The most important pursuit for all Christians, individually and corporately, is holiness. The first mission of the church is to honor and glorify God, and He can be honored and glorified by His children only as they grow to be like Him in character. Although evangelism is the cutting edge of the church's ministry, holiness is the only foundation on which effective evangelism or any other ministry can be built. The supreme priority of the church is holiness, purity of inward life. God can accomplish whatever He desires through a believer or a church that is holy, but He can do little through one that is not.

REFLECTING ON THE TEXT

8) How can walking in the Spirit by God's grace lead to living a more holy life?

By walking in the Spirit you are demonstrating in action your inward holiness.

115

9) In what areas of your life (or ministry) are you tempted to give up out of weariness, or out of a sense that your efforts aren't making a difference? What counsel would Paul give you?

I think in my sin life. The consequences seem unreal or not tangible. There's more immediate reward.

10) When was the last time you pondered the mystery and majesty of all that the cross of Christ represents? Express here your gratitude to God for His amazing blessings that were poured out on you because of the cross.

It's been a long time since I've poured out or experienced his majesty and truly been grateful. Doing so right now seems a little contrived and superficial. Perhaps

PERSONAL RESPONSE

Write out additional reflections, questions you may have, or a prayer.

I'm not fully in the spirit. and seeing this exercise as an obligation?

116

ADDITIONAL NOTES

Additional Notes

Additional Notes

ADDITIONAL NOTES

Look for these exciting titles by John MacArthur

Experiencing the Passion of Christ

Experiencing the Passion of Christ Student Edition

Twelve Extraordinary Women Workbook

Twelve Ordinary Men Workbook

Welcome to the Family:
What to Expect Now That You're a Christian

What the Bible Says About Parenting:
Biblical Principles for Raising Godly Children

Hard to Believe Workbook:
The High Cost and Infinite Value of Following Jesus

The John MacArthur Study Library for PDA

The MacArthur Bible Commentary

The MacArthur Study Bible, NKJV

The MacArthur Topical Bible, NKJV

The MacArthur Bible Commentary

The MacArthur Bible Handbook

The MacArthur Bible Studies series

Available at your local Christian Bookstore
or visit www.thomasnelson.com

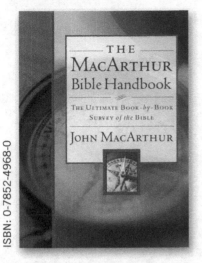